WATER BY THE SPOONFUL

BY QUIARA ALEGRÍA HUDES

★

★

DRAMATISTS
PLAY SERVICE
INC.

For Ray Beauchamp

ACKNOWLEDGMENTS

This play, its story, and its characters are works of fiction. However, I owe a debt of gratitude to Othet Sauris and Elliot Ruiz, whom I interviewed before writing. Without their generosity of story and spirit, my imagination would not have landed at this play.

More seeds of inspiration came from interviews with Jeremy Cohen, Sandy Moehle, Rik Albani, and Alan Leshner. Roger Zepernick, my dear friend, contributed to Scene 10 by sending me a transcript of a speech he gave in Philadelphia, along with his permission to adapt it.

Gratitude to all my family, with a special beam of light shining on my mother, Virginia Sanchez. Linda Hudes, Eugenia Burgos, and Liz Morales provide ongoing support and inspiration. My siblings keep me young at heart: Gabriela Sanchez, Ariel Hudes, and Forrest Hudes. My stepfather, Mercedes Sanchez, told me a tale of his first cold drink. My father, Henry Hudes, sanded the curly maple of my writing desk.

Gratitude to my collaborators. John Buzzetti, your joy is infectious. Michael Wilson, what a champion you are. Davis McCallum, Armando Riesco, and Zabryna Guevara — what shall we call our theater company? Hana Sharif and Darko Tresnjak, for steel-beam support at Hartford Stage. Catherine Rush, for drawing the starting line, and Kent Gash, for grabbing the baton along the way. New Dramatists, for seven years of safe space.

Gratitude, ongoing, to Paula Vogel.

Gratitude, endless, to Ray.

WATER BY THE SPOONFUL was originally commissioned and produced by Hartford Stage (Michael Wilson, Artistic Director [outgoing]; Darko Tresnjak, Artistic Director [incoming]; Michael Stotts, Managing Director) in Hartford, Connecticut, opening on October 26, 2011. It was directed by Davis McCallum; the set design was by Neil Patel; the costume design was by Chloe Chapin; the lighting design was by Russell H. Champa; the sound design was by Bray Poor; the original music was by J. Michael Friedman; the production stage manager was Megan Schwarz Dickert; and the production manager was Bryan T. Holcombe. The cast was as follows:

ELLIOT .... Armando Riesco
ODESSA .... Liza Colón-Zayas
YAZMIN .... Zabryna Guevara
CHUTES&LADDERS .... Ray Anthony
FOUNTAINHEAD .... Matthew Boston
PROFESSOR AMAN/GHOST .... Demosthenes Chrysan
ORANGUTAN .... Teresa Avia Lim

WATER BY THE SPOONFUL received its New York premiere at Second Stage Theatre (Carole Rothman, Artistic Director; Casey Reitz, Executive Director) in December 2012. It was directed by Davis McCallum; the set design was by Neil Patel; the costume design was by ESosa; the lighting design was by Russell H. Champa; the sound design was by Joshua Schmidt; the projection design was by Aaron Rhyne; the fight director was Thomas Schall; the production stage manager was Roy Harris; the stage manager was Trisha Henson; and the production manager was Jeff Wild. The cast was as follows:

ELLIOT .... Armando Riesco
ODESSA .... Liza Colón-Zayas
YAZMIN .... Zabryna Guevara
CHUTES&LADDERS .... Ray Anthony
FOUNTAINHEAD .... Bill Heck
POLICEMAN/PROFESSOR AMAN/GHOST ... Ryan Shams
ORANGUTAN .... Sue Jean Kim

CHARACTERS

ODESSA ORTIZ, 39, a.k.a. Haikumom, founder of www.recover together.com, works odd janitorial jobs, lives one notch above squalor.

ELLIOT ORTIZ, 24, an Iraq vet with a slight limp, works at Subway Hoagies, scores an occasional job as a model or actor, Yazmin's cousin, Odessa's birth son.

YAZMIN ORTIZ, 31, adjunct professor of music, Odessa's niece and Elliot's cousin.

FOUNTAINHEAD, 38, a.k.a. John, a computer programmer and entrepreneur, lives on Philadelphia's Main Line, white.

CHUTES&LADDERS, 56, lives in San Diego, has worked a low-level job at the IRS since the Reagan years, African-American, his real name is Clayton "Buddy" Wilkie.

ORANGUTAN, 31, a recent community college graduate, Japanese by birth, her real name is Madeleine Mays and before that Yoshiko Sakai.

A GHOST, also plays PROFESSOR AMAN, an Arabic professor at Swarthmore; also plays A POLICEMAN in Japan.

TIME

2009. Six years after Elliot left for Iraq.

PLACE

Philadelphia, San Diego, Japan, and Puerto Rico.

SET

The stage has two worlds. The "real world" is populated with chairs. The chairs are from many locations — living rooms, an office, a seminar room, a church, a diner, internet cafes. They all have the worn-in feel of life. A duct-taped La-Z-Boy. Salvaged trash chairs. A busted-up metal folding chair from a rec center. An Aero chair. An Eames chair. A chair/desk from a college classroom. Diner chairs. A chair from an internet café in Japan. Living room chairs. Library chairs. A church pew. Facing in all different directions.

The "online world" is an empty space. A space that connects the chairs.

MUSIC

Jazz. Sublime stuff like John Coltrane's *A Love Supreme*. And noise, like his later *Ascension* or other free jazz.

NOTE

Unless specifically noted, when characters are online, don't have actors typing on a keyboard. Treat it like regular conversation rather than the act of writing or typing. They can be doing things people do in the comfort of their home like eating potato chips, walking around in jammies, cooking, doing dishes, clipping nails, etc.

WATER BY THE SPOONFUL

Scene 1

Swarthmore College. Elliot and Yaz eat breakfast. Elliot wears a Subway Hoagies polo shirt.

ELLIOT. This guy ain't coming. How do you know him?

YAZ. We're on a committee together.

ELLIOT. My shift starts in fifteen.

YAZ. Alright, we'll go.

ELLIOT. Five more minutes. Tonight on the way home, we gotta stop by Whole Foods.

YAZ. Sure, I need toothpaste.

ELLIOT. Yaz, you gotta help me with my mom.

YAZ. You said she had a good morning.

ELLIOT. She cooked breakfast.

YAZ. Progress.

ELLIOT. No. The docs said she can't be eating all that junk, it'll mess with her chemo, so she crawls out of bed for the first time in days and cooks eggs for breakfast. In two inches of pork chop fat. I'm like, Mom, recycle glass and plastic, not grease. She thinks putting the egg on top of a paper towel after you cook it makes it healthy. I told her, Mom, you gotta cook egg whites. In Pam spray. But it has to be her way. Like, "That's how we ate them in Puerto Rico and we turned out fine." You gotta talk to her. I'm trying to teach her about quinoa. Broccoli rabe. Healthy shit. So I get home the other day, she had made quinoa with bacon. She was like, "It's healthy!"

YAZ. That's Ginny. The more stubborn she's being, the better she's feeling.

ELLIOT. I gave those eggs to the dogs when she went to the bathroom. *(She pulls some papers from her purse.)*

YAZ. You wanna be my witness?

ELLIOT. To what? *(Yaz signs the papers.)*

YAZ. My now-legal failure. I'm divorced.

ELLIOT. Yaz. I don't want to hear that.

YAZ. You've been saying that for months and I've been keeping my mouth closed. I just need a John Hancock.

ELLIOT. What happened to "trial separation"?

YAZ. There was a verdict. William fell out of love with me.

ELLIOT. I've never seen you two argue.

YAZ. We did, we just had smiles on our faces.

ELLIOT. That's bullshit. You don't divorce someone before you even have a fight with them. I'm calling him.

YAZ. Go ahead.

ELLIOT. He was just texting me about going to the Phillies game on Sunday.

YAZ. So, go. He didn't fall out of love with the family, just me.

ELLIOT. I'm going to ask him who he's been screwing behind your back.

YAZ. No one, Elliot.

ELLIOT. You were tappin' some extra on the side?

YAZ. He woke up one day and I was the same as any other person passing by on the street, and life is short, and you can only live in mediocrity so long.

ELLIOT. You two are the dog and the owner that look like each other. Y'all are *The Cosby Show.* Conundrum, Yaz and William make a funny, end of episode. You show all us cousins, maybe we can't ever do it ourselves, but it is possible.

YAZ. Did I ever say, "It's possible"?

ELLIOT. By example.

YAZ. Did I ever say those words? *(Professor Aman enters.)*

AMAN. Yazmin, forgive me. You must be …

ELLIOT. Elliot Ortiz. Nice to meet you, I appreciate it.

AMAN. Professor Aman. *(They shake.)* We'll have to make this short and sweet, my lecture begins … began … well, talk fast.

ELLIOT. Yaz, give us a second?

YAZ. I'll be in the car. *(Exits.)*

ELLIOT. I'm late, too, so …

AMAN. You need something translated.

ELLIOT. Just a phrase. Thanks, man.

AMAN. Eh, your sister's cute.

ELLIOT. Cousin. I wrote it phonetically. You grow up speaking Arabic?

AMAN. English. What's your native tongue?

ELLIOT. Spanglish. *(Hands Aman a piece of paper.)*

AMAN. *Mom-ken men fad-luck ted-dini ga-waz saf-far-i. Momken men-fadluck ted-dini gawaz saffari.* Am I saying that right?

ELLIOT. *(Spooked.)* Spot on.

AMAN. You must have some familiarity with Arabic to remember it so clearly.

ELLIOT. Maybe I heard it on TV or something.

AMAN. An odd phrase.

ELLIOT. It's like a song I can't get out of my head.

AMAN. Yazmin didn't tell me what this is for.

ELLIOT. It's not for anything.

AMAN. Do you mind me asking, what's around your neck?

ELLIOT. Something my girl gave me.

AMAN. Can I see? *(Elliot pulls dog tags from under his shirt.)* Romantic gift. You were in the Army.

ELLIOT. Marines.

AMAN. Iraq?

ELLIOT. For a minute.

AMAN. Were you reluctant to tell me that?

ELLIOT. No.

AMAN. Still in the service?

ELLIOT. Honorable discharge. Leg injury.

AMAN. When?

ELLIOT. A few years ago.

AMAN. This is a long time to have a phrase stuck in your head.

ELLIOT. What is this, man?

AMAN. You tell me.

ELLIOT. It's just a phrase. If you don't want to translate, just say so.

AMAN. A college buddy is making a film about Marines in Iraq. Gritty, documentary-style. He's looking for some veterans to interview. Get an authentic point of view. Maybe I could pass your number onto him.

ELLIOT. Nope. No interviews for this guy.

AMAN. You're asking me for a favor. *(Pause.)* Yazmin told me you're an actor. Every actor needs a break, right?

ELLIOT. I did enough Q and A's about the service. People manipulate you with the questions.

AMAN. It's not just to interview. He needs a right-hand man, an expert to help him. How do Marines hold a gun? How do they kick in civilian doors, this sort of thing. How do they say "Ooh rah" in a patriotic manner?

ELLIOT. Are you his headhunter or something?

AMAN. I'm helping with the translations, I have a small stake and I want the movie to be accurate. And you seem not unintelligent. For a maker of sandwiches. *(Hands him a business card.)* He's in L.A. In case you want a career change. I give you a cup of sugar, you give me a cup of sugar.

ELLIOT. If I have a minute, I'll dial the digits. *(Takes the business card.)* So what's it mean?

AMAN. *Momken men-fadluck ted-dini gawaz saffari.* Rough translation, "Can I please have my passport back?"

Scene 2

Odessa's living room and kitchen. She makes coffee. She goes over to her computer, clicks a button. On a screen we see an icon of a waterfall: HAIKUMOM, SITEADMIN, STATUS: ONLINE.

HAIKUMOM. Rise and shine, kiddos, the rooster's a-crowin', it's a beautiful day to be sober. *(No response.)* Your Thursday morning haiku:

if you get restless

buy a hydrangea or rose

water it, wait, bloom.

(Odessa continues making coffee. A computer dings and on another screen we see an icon of an orangutan: ORANGUTAN, STATUS: ONLINE.)

ORANGUTAN. Ninety-one days. Smiley face.

HAIKUMOM. *(Relieved.)* Orangutan! Jesus, I thought my primate friend had disappeared back to the jungle.

ORANGUTAN. Disappeared? Yes. Jungle? Happily, no.

HAIKUMOM. I'm trying to put a high-five emoticon but my computer is being a capital B. So, high five! *(They high five in the air. Another computer screen lights up with an icon of a game board: CHUTES&LADDERS, STATUS: ONLINE.)*

CHUTES&LADDERS. Orangutan? I was about to send a search party after your rear end. Kid, log on. No news is bad news.

ORANGUTAN. Chutes&Ladders, giving me a hard time as usual. I'd expect nothing less.

CHUTES&LADDERS. Your last post says, "Day One. Packing bags, gotta run," and then you don't log on for three months?

ORANGUTAN. I was going to Japan, I had to figure out what shoes to bring.

HAIKUMOM. The country?

CHUTES&LADDERS. What happened to Maine?

ORANGUTAN. And I quote, "Get a hobby, find a new job, an exciting city, go teach English in a foreign country." Did you guys think I wouldn't take your seasoned advice? I was batting 0 for ten, and for the first time, guys, I feel fucking free.

HAIKUMOM. *(Non-judgmental.)* Censored.

ORANGUTAN. I wake up and I think, "What's the world got up its sleeve today?" and I look forward to the answer. So, thank you.

CHUTES&LADDERS. We told you so.

ORANGUTAN. *(Playful.)* Shut up.

HAIKUMOM. You're welcome.

ORANGUTAN. I gave my parents the URL. My username, my password. They logged on and read every post I've ever put on here and for once they said they understood. They had completely cut me off but after reading this site they bought me the plane ticket. One way. I teach English in the mornings. I have a class of children, a class of teens, and a class of adults, most of whom are older than me. I am free in the afternoons. I have a paycheck which I use for legal things like ice cream, noodles, and socks. I walk around feeling like maybe I am normal. Maybe, just possibly, I'm not that different. Or maybe it's just homeland delusions.

CHUTES&LADDERS and HAIKUMOM. Homeland?

HAIKUMOM. You're Japanese?

ORANGUTAN. I was, for the first eight days of my life. Yoshiko Sakai. Then on day nine I was adopted and moved to Cape Lewiston, Maine, where I became Ma — M.M., and where in all my days I have witnessed one other Asian. In the Superfresh. Deli counter.

CHUTES&LADDERS. Japan ... Wow, that little white rock sure doesn't discriminate.

HAIKUMOM. Amen.

ORANGUTAN. Mango Internet Café. I'm sitting in an orange plastic chair, a little view of the Hokkaido waterfront.

HAIKUMOM. Japan has a waterfront?

CHUTES&LADDERS. It's an island.

HAIKUMOM. Really? Are there beaches? Can you go swimming?

ORANGUTAN. The ocean reminds me of Maine. Cold water, very quiet, fisherman, boats, the breeze. I wouldn't try swimming. I'm just a looker. I was never one to actually have an experience.

CHUTES&LADDERS. Ah, the ocean ... There's only one thing on this planet I'm more scared of than that big blue lady.

HAIKUMOM. Let me guess: landing on a sliding board square?

CHUTES&LADDERS. LOL, truer words have never been spoken. You know I was born just a few miles from the Pacific. In the fresh salt air. Back in "those days" I'm at Coronado Beach with a few "friends" doing my "thing" and I get sucked up under this wave. I gasp, I breathe in and my lungs fill with water. I'm like, this is it, I'm going to meet my maker. I had never felt so heavy, not even during my two OD's. I was sinking to the bottom and my head hit the sand like a lead ball. My body just felt like an anvil. The next thing I know there's fingers digging in my ankles. This lifeguard pulls me out, I'm throwing up salt water. I say to him, "Hey blondie, you don't know me from Adam but you are my witness: Today's the day I start to live." And this lifeguard, I mean he was young with these muscles, this kid looks at me like, "Who is this big black dude who can't even doggy paddle?" When I stand up and brush the sand off me, people applaud. An old lady touches my cheek and says, "I thought you were done for." I get back to San Diego that night, make one phone call, the next day I'm in my first meeting, sitting in a folding chair, saying the Serenity Prayer.

ORANGUTAN. I hate to inflate your already swollen ego, but that was a lucid, touching story. By the way, did you get the lifeguard's name? He sounds hot.

HAIKUMOM. Hey Chutes&Ladders, it's never too late to learn. Most Y.M.C.A.'s offer adult swimming classes.

CHUTES&LADDERS. I'll do the world a favor and stay out of a Speedo.

ORANGUTAN. Sober air toast. To lifeguards.

CHUTES&LADDERS and HAIKUMOM. To lifeguards.
ORANGUTAN, CHUTES&LADDERS and HAIKUMOM.
Clink.
HAIKUMOM. Chutes&Ladders, I'm buying you a pair of water
wings.

Scene 3

Music like John Coltrane's A Love Supreme *plays.* * *A Subway
Hoagie shop on Philadelphia's Main Line. Elliot sits behind the
counter. The phone rings. He gets up, hobbles to it — he walks
with a limp.*

ELLIOT. Subway Main Line. Lar! Laaar, what's it doing for you
today? Staying in the shade? I got you, how many you need? Listen,
the delivery guy's out and my little sports injury is giving me hell so
can you pick up? Cool, sorry for the inconvenience. Let me grab a
pen. A'ight, pick a hoagie, any hoagie! *(Elliot begins writing the order.
Lights rise to a seminar room at Swarthmore College. We find Yaz mid-
class. She hits a button on a stereo and the music stops playing.)*
YAZ. [Coltrane's *A Love Supreme*, 1964.*] Dissonance is still a
gateway to resolution. A B-diminished chord is still resolving to?
Class? C-major. A tritone is still resolving up to? The major sixth.
Diminished chords, tritones, still didn't have the right to be their
own independent thought. In 1965 something changed. The
ugliness bore no promise of a happy ending. The ugliness became
an end in itself. Coltrane democratized the notes. He said, they're
all equal. Freedom. It was called Free Jazz but freedom is a hard
thing to express musically without spinning into noise. [This is
from *Ascension*, 1965.*] *(She plays some free jazz. It sounds uglier
than the first sample. In the Subway shop, a figure comes into view.
It is The Ghost.)*
GHOST. *Momken men-fadluck ted-dini gawaz saffari? (Elliot tries
to ignore The Ghost, reading off the order.)*

---

* See Special Note on Songs and Recordings on copyright page.

ELLIOT. That's three teriyaki onion with chicken. First with hots and onions. Second with everything. Third with extra bacon. Two spicy Italian with American cheese on whole grain. One BMT on flatbread. Good so far?

GHOST. *Momken men-fadluck ted-dini gawaz saffari?*

ELLIOT. Five chocolate chip cookies, one oatmeal raisin. Three Baked Lays, three Doritos. Two Sprite Zeros, one Barq's, one Coke, two orange sodas. How'd I do?

GHOST. *Momken men-fadluck ted-dini gawaz saffari?*

ELLIOT. Alright, that'll be ready in fifteen minutes. One sec for your total. *(Elliot gets a text message. He reads it, his entire demeanor shifts.)* Lar, I just got a text. There's a family emergency, I can't do this order right now. *(Elliot hangs up. He exits, limping away.)*

YAZ. Oh come on, don't make that face. I know it feels academic. You're going to leave here and become R&B hit makers and Sondheim clones and never think about this noise again. But this is Coltrane, people, this is not Schoenberg! This is jazz, stuff people listen to *voluntarily*. Shopping period is still on, go sit in one session of "Germans and Noise" down the hall and you'll come running back begging for this muzak. *(Yaz turns off the music.)* In fact, change the syllabus. No listening report next week. Instead, I want you to pinpoint the first time you really noticed dissonance. The composer, the piece, the measures. Two pages analyzing the notes and two pages describing the experience personally. This is your creation myth. Before you leave this school you better figure out that story and cling to it for dear life or you'll be a stockbroker within a year. I was thirteen, I worked in a corrugated box factory all summer, I saved up enough to find my first music teacher — up to that point I was self-taught, playing to the radio. I walked into Don Rappaport's room at Settlement Music School. He was old, he had jowls, he was sitting at the piano and he said, "What do you do?" I said, "I'm a composer, sir." Presumptuous, right? I sat down and played Mr. Rappaport a Yazmin original. He said, "It's pretty, everything goes together. It's like an outfit where your socks are blue and your pants, shirt, hat are all blue." Then he said, "Play an F-sharp major in your left hand." Then he said, "Play a C-major in your right hand." "Now play them together." He asked me, "Does it go together?" I told him, "No, sir." He said, "Now go home and write." My first music lesson was seven minutes long. I had never really heard dissonance before. *(Yaz's phone vibrates. She sees the*

16

caller with concern.) Let's take five. *(As students file out, Yaz makes a phone call. Lights up on Elliot outside the Subway Hoagie shop.)*

YAZ. *("What's the bad news?")* You called three times.

ELLIOT. She's still alive.

YAZ. Okay.

ELLIOT. Jefferson Hospital. They admitted her three hours ago, Pop had the courtesy to text me.

YAZ. Are you still at work?

ELLIOT. Just smashed the bathroom mirror all over the floor. Boss sent me out to the parking lot.

YAZ. Wait there. I'm on my way.

ELLIOT. "Your mom is on breathing machine." Who texts that? Who texts that and then doesn't pick up the phone?

YAZ. I'll be there within twenty.

ELLIOT. Why did I come to work today?

YAZ. She had a good morning. You wanted your thing translated.

ELLIOT. She cooked and I wouldn't eat a bite off the fork. There's a Subway hoagies around the corner and I had to work half an hour away.

YAZ. You didn't want your buddies to see you working a normal job.

ELLIOT. Not normal job. Shit job. I'm a butler. A porter of sandwiches.

YAZ. Ginny's been to Hades and back, stronger each time.

ELLIOT. What is Hades?

YAZ. In Greek mythology, the river through the underworld—

ELLIOT. My mom's on a machine and you're dropping vocab words?! *(A ding.)*

YAZ. Text message, don't hang up. *(She looks at her phone. A moment, then.)* You still there?

ELLIOT. It was my dad, wasn't it? Yaz, spit it out.

YAZ. It was your dad.

ELLIOT. And? Yaz, I'm about to start walking down Lancaster Avenue for thirty miles 'til I get back to Philly and I don't care if I snap every wire out my leg and back I need to get out of here. I need to see Mom, I need to talk to her!

YAZ. He said, "Waiting for Elliot 'til we turn off the machine."

Scene 4

The chat room. A screen lights up: We see an "anonymous male" icon: FOUNTAINHEAD, STATUS: ONLINE.

FOUNTAINHEAD. I've uh, wow, hello there everyone. Delete, delete. Good afternoon. Evening. Delete. *(Deep breath.)* Things I am taking: My life into my own hands. My gorgeous, deserving wife out for our seventh anniversary. Me: Mildly athletic, but work twice as hard. Won state for javelin two years straight. Ran a half-marathon last fall. Animated arguer. Two medals for undergrad debate. M.B.A. from Wharton. Beautiful wife, two sons. Built a programming company from the ground up, featured in the New York *Times* Circuits section, sold it at its peak, bought a yellow Porsche, got a day job to keep myself honest. Salary was 300K, company was run by morons, got laid off, handsome severance, which left me swimming in cash and free time. Me and crack: long story short, I was at a conference with our C.F.O. and two programmers and a not-unattractive lady in H.R. They snorted, invited me to join. A few weeks later that little rock waltzed right into my hand. I've been using off-and-on since. One eightball every Saturday, strict rations, portion control. Though the last three or four weeks, it's less like getting high and more like trying to build a time machine. Anything to get back the romance of that virgin smoke. Last weekend I let myself buy more than my predetermined allotment—I buy in small quantity, because as with my food, I eat what's on my plate. Anyway, I ran over a curb, damaged the underside of my Porsche. Now it's in the shop and I'm driving a rental Mustang. So, not rock bottom but a rental Ford is as close to rock bottom as I'd like to get. Fast forward to tonight. I'm watching my wife's eyelids fall and telling myself, "You are on punishment, Poppa. Daddy's on time out. Do not get out of bed, do not tiptoe down those stairs, do not go down to that basement, do not sit beside that foosball table, do not smoke, and please do not crawl on the carpet looking for one last hit in the fibers." *(Pause.)* In kindergarten my son tested into G&T. Gifted and talented. You meet with the school, they tailor the program to the kid. Math, reading, art, whatever the parent chooses. I said, "Teach my son how to learn." How to use a library. How to find original source material, read a map, track down the experts so he becomes the expert. Which gets me to — You: the experts. It's the first day of school and I'm knocking at your classroom door. I got my Number Two pencils, I'll sit in the front row, pay attention, and do my homework. No lesson is too basic. Teach me every technique. Any tip so that Saturday doesn't become every day. Any actions that keep you in the driver seat. Healthy habits and rational thoughts to blot out that voice in the back of my head. Today, I quit. My wife cannot know, she'd get suspicious if I were at meetings all the time. There can be no medical records, so therapy is out. At least it's not heroin, I'm not facing a physical war. It's a psychological battle and I'm armed with two weapons: willpower and the experts. I'm taking my wife out tomorrow for our seventh anniversary and little does she know that when we clink glasses, I'll be toasting to Day One. *(Odessa is emotional. Chutes&Ladders and Orangutan seem awestruck.)*

ORANGUTAN. *(Clapping.)* That was brave.

CHUTES&LADDERS. What. The.

HAIKUMOM. Careful.

CHUTES&LADDERS. Fuck.

HAIKUMOM. Censored.

ORANGUTAN. I'm making popcorn. Oh, this is gonna be fun!

CHUTES&LADDERS. Fountainhead, speaking of experts, I've been meaning to become an asshole. Can you teach me how?

HAIKUMOM. Censored!

ORANGUTAN. "Tips?" This isn't a cooking website. And what is a half-marathon?

CHUTES&LADDERS. Maybe it's something like a half-crack addict. Or a half-husband.

ORANGUTAN. Was that an addiction coming out or an online dating profile? "Married Male Dope Fiend. Smokin' hot."

CHUTES&LADDERS. Fountainhead, you sound like the kind of guy who's read *The Seven Habits of Highly Effective People* cover to cover. Was one of those habits crack? Give the essays a rest and type three words. "I'm. A. Crackhead."

ORANGUTAN. You know, Adderall is like totes cool. Us crackheads, we're like yucky and stuff. We're like so '90s. Go try the Adderall edge!

HAIKUMOM. Hey.

ORANGUTAN. The guy's a hoax. Twenty bucks says he's pranking. Let's start a new thread.

HAIKUMOM. Hi, Fountainhead, welcome. As the site administrator, I want to honestly congratulate you for accomplishing what so many addicts only hope for: one clean day. Any time you feel like using, log on here instead. It's worked for me. When it comes to junkies, I dug lower than the dungeon. Once upon a time I had a beautiful family, too. Now all I have is six years clean. Don't lose what I lost, what Chutes&Ladders lost.

CHUTES&LADDERS. Excuse me.

HAIKUMOM. Orangutan, I just checked and Fountainhead has no aliases and has never logged onto this site before under a different pseudonym, which are the usual markers of a scam.

ORANGUTAN. I'm just saying. Who toasts to their first day of sobriety?

CHUTES&LADDERS. I hope it's seltzer in that there champagne glass.

ORANGUTAN. Ginger ale, Shirley Temple.

CHUTES&LADDERS. "A toast, honey. I had that seven-year-itch so I became a crackhead."

CHUTES&LADDERS and ORANGUTAN. Clink.

HAIKUMOM. Hey, kiddos. Your smiley administrator doesn't want to start purging messages. For rules of the forums click on this link. No personal attacks.

ORANGUTAN. We don't come to this site for a pat on the back.

HAIKUMOM. I'm just saying. R-e-s-p-e-c-t.

CHUTES&LADDERS. I will always give crack the respect it deserves. Some purebred poodle comes pissing on my tree trunk? Damn straight I'll chase his ass out my forest.

HAIKUMOM. This here is my forest. You two think you were all humble pie when you started out? Check your original posts.

ORANGUTAN. Oh, I know mine. "I-am-scared-I-will-kill-myself-talk-me-off-the-ledge."

HAIKUMOM. So unless someone gets that desperate they don't deserve our noble company? "Suffer like me, or you ain't legit?"

ORANGUTAN. Haikumom's growing claws.

HAIKUMOM. Just don't act entitled because you got so low. *(To Fountainhead.)* Sorry. Fountainhead, forgive us. We get very passionate because —

CHUTES&LADDERS. Fountainhead, your Porsche has a massive engine. You got bulging marathon muscles. I'm sure your penis is as big as that javelin you used to throw.

HAIKUMOM. Censored.

CHUTES&LADDERS. But none of those things come close to the size of your ego. If you can put that aside, you may, *may* stand a chance. Otherwise, you're fucked, my friend.

HAIKUMOM. Message purged.

ORANGUTAN. OH MY GOD, WE'RE DYING HERE, DO WE HAVE TO BE SO POLITE ABOUT IT?

HAIKUMOM. Censored.

ORANGUTAN. Oh my G-zero-D. Democracy or dictatorship?

CHUTES&LADDERS. Hey Fountainhead, why the silence? *(Fountainhead logs off.)*

HAIKUMOM. Nice work, guys. Congratulations.

CHUTES&LADDERS. You don't suppose he's ... crawling on the carpet looking for one last rock?

ORANGUTAN. Lordy lord lord, I'm about to go over his house and start looking for one myself!

HAIKUMOM. That's why you're in Japan, little monkey. For now, I'm closing this thread. Fountainhead, if you want to reopen it, email me directly.

Scene 5

A flower shop in Center City Philadelphia. Yaz looks over some brochures. Elliot enters, his limp looking worse.

YAZ. I was starting to get worried. How you holding?

ELLIOT. Joe's Gym, perfect remedy.

YAZ. You went boxing? Really?

ELLIOT. I had to blow off steam. Women don't get it.

YAZ. Don't be a pig. You've had four leg surgeries, no more boxing.

ELLIOT. Did Odessa call?

YAZ. You know how she is. Shutting herself out from the world.

ELLIOT. We need help this week.

21

YAZ. And I got your back.

ELLIOT. I'm just saying, pick up the phone and ask, "Do you need anything, Elliot?"

YAZ. I did speak to your dad. Everyone's gathering at the house. People start arriving from P.R. in a few hours. The next-door neighbor brought over two trays of pigs' feet.

ELLIOT. I just threw up in my mouth.

YAZ. Apparently a fight broke out over who gets your mom's pocketbooks.

ELLIOT. Those pleather things from the ten dollar store?

YAZ. Thank you, it's not like she had Gucci purses!

ELLIOT. People just need to manufacture drama.

YAZ. He said they were tearing through Ginny's closets like it was a shopping spree. "I want this necklace!" "I want the photo album!" "Yo, those *chancletas* are mine!" I'm like, damn, let Ginny be buried first.

ELLIOT. Yo, let's spend the day here.

YAZ. *(Handing him some papers.)* Brochures. I was being indecisive so the florist went to work on a wedding bouquet. I ruled out seven, you make the final call. Celebration of Life, Blooming Garden, Eternity Wreath.

ELLIOT. All of those have carnations. I don't want a carnation within a block of the church.

YAZ. You told me to eliminate seven. I eliminated seven. Close your eyes and point.

ELLIOT. Am I a particularly demanding person?

YAZ. Yes. What's so wrong with a carnation?

ELLIOT. You know what a carnation says to the world? That they were out of roses at the 7-Eleven. It should look something like Mom's garden.

YAZ. *(In agreement.)* Graveside Remembrances? That looks something like it … I'm re-nominating Graveside Remembrances. Putting it back on the table.

ELLIOT. You couldn't find anything tropical? Yaz, you could find a needle in a damn haystack and you couldn't find a bird-of-paradise or something?

YAZ. He just shoved some brochures in my hand.

ELLIOT. *(Stares her down.)* You have an awful poker face.

YAZ. Now, look here.

ELLIOT. You did find something.

YAZ. No. Not exactly.

ELLIOT. How much does it cost? Yaz, this is my mom we're talking about.

YAZ. Five hundred more. Just for the casket piece.

ELLIOT. You can't lie for shit, you never could.

YAZ. Orchid Paradise. *(Yaz hands him another brochure. They look at it together.)*

ELLIOT. Aw, damn. Damn. That looks like mom's garden.

YAZ. Spitting image.

ELLIOT. *(Pointing.)* I think she grew those.

YAZ. Right next to the tomatoes.

ELLIOT. But hers were yellow. Fuck.

YAZ. It's very odd to order flowers when someone dies. Because the flowers are just gonna die, too. "Would you like some death with your death?"

ELLIOT. *(A confession.)* I didn't water them.

YAZ. *(Getting it.)* What, are you supposed to be a gardener all of a sudden?

ELLIOT. It doesn't rain for a month and do I grab the hose and water mom's garden one time?

YAZ. You were feeding her. Giving her meds. Bathing her. I could've come over and watered a leaf. A single petal.

ELLIOT. The last four days, she'd wake me up in the middle of the night. "Did you water the flowers?" "Yeah, Mom, just like you told me to yesterday." "Carry me out back, I want to see." "Mom, you're too heavy, I can't carry you down those steps one more time today."

YAZ. Little white lies.

ELLIOT. Can you do the sermon?

YAZ. This is becoming a second career.

ELLIOT. Because you're the only one who doesn't cry.

YAZ. Unlike Julia.

ELLIOT. *(Imitating.)* "Ay dios mio! Ay! Ay!"

YAZ. I hate public speaking.

ELLIOT. You're a teacher.

YAZ. It's different when it's ideas. Talking about ideas isn't saying something, it's making syllables with your mouth.

ELLIOT. You love ideas. All you ever wanted to do was have ideas.

YAZ. It was an elaborate bait and switch. The ideas don't fill the void, they just help you articulate it.

ELLIOT. You've spoken at City Hall. On the radio.

YAZ. You're the face of Main Line Chevrolet. *(Pause.)* Can I do it in English?

ELLIOT. You could do it in Russian for all I care. I'll just be in the front row acting like my cheek is itchy so no one sees me crying.

YAZ. The elders want a good Spanish sermon.

ELLIOT. Mami Ginny was it. You're the elder now.

YAZ. I'm 31.

ELLIOT. But you don't look a day over fifty.

YAZ. You gotta do me a favor in return. I know this is your tragedy but … Call William. Ask him not to come to the funeral.

ELLIOT. Oh shit.

YAZ. He saw the obit in the *Daily News.*

ELLIOT. They were close. Mami Ginny loved that blonde hair. She was the *madrina* of your wedding.

YAZ. William relinquished mourning privileges. You fall out of love with me, you lose certain rights. He calls talking about, "I want the condo." That I decorated, that I painted. "Oh, and where's the funeral, by the way?" You know, he's been to four funerals in the Ortiz clan and I could feel it, there was a part of him, under it all, that was disgusted. The open casket. The prayers.

ELLIOT. It is disgusting.

YAZ. Sitting in the pew knowing what freaks we are.

ELLIOT. He's good people.

YAZ. Truth is, I was at his side doing the same thing, acting like I'm removed, that I'm somehow different.

ELLIOT. Hey, hey, done.

YAZ. One more condition. I go to Puerto Rico with you. We scatter her ashes together.

ELLIOT. Mami Ginny couldn't be buried in Philly. She had to have her ashes thrown at a waterfall in El Yunque, just to be the most Puerto Rican motherfucker around.

YAZ. I saw your Colgate ad.

ELLIOT. Dang, cousin Yaz watches Spanish TV?

YAZ. Shut up.

ELLIOT. I walked into the casting office, flashed my pearly whites, showed them my military I.D. and I charmed them.

YAZ. Do it.

ELLIOT. Give me a dollar.

YAZ. For that big cheeseburger smile? *(She gives him a dollar.)*

ELLIOT. *(Smiling.)* "*Sonrisa,* baby!" *(Yaz cracks up laughing, which devolves into tears.)* How we gonna pay for Orchid Paradise?

YAZ. They should have a frequent flower card. They punch a hole. Buy nine funeral bouquets, get the tenth free. We'd be living in a house full of lilies. Look at that guy. Arranging his daisies like little treasures. What do you think it's like to be him? To be normal?

ELLIOT. Normal? A hundred bucks says that dude has a closet full of animal porno at home.

YAZ. I bet in his family funerals are rare occasions. I bet he's never seen a cousin get arrested. Let alone one under the age of eighteen. I bet he never saw his eight-year-old cousin sipping rum through a twisty straw or … I just remembered this time cousin Maria was babysitting me …

ELLIOT. Fat Maria or bucktooth Maria?

YAZ. I was dyeing her hair. I had never dyed hair before so I asked her to read me the next step and she handed me the box and said, "You read it." And I said, "My rubber gloves are covered in toxic goop, I can't really hold that right now." And so she held it in front of my eyes and said, "You gonna have to read it because I sure as hell can't."

ELLIOT. I been knowed that.

YAZ. I said, "But you graduated from high school." She said, "They just pass you, I just stood in the back." I was in fourth grade. I could read! *(Pause.)* I have a degree written in Latin that I don't even understand. I paid seventeen thousand dollars for my piano.

ELLIOT. Oh shit.

YAZ. I have a mortgage on my piano. Drive two miles north? William told me every time I went to North Philly, I'd come back different. His family has Quaker Oats for DNA. They play Pictionary on New Year's. I'd sit there wishing I could scoop the blood out my veins like you scoop the seeds out a pumpkin and he'd be like, "Whatchu thinking about, honey?" and I'd be like, "Nothing. Let's play some Pictionary."

ELLIOT. Yo, being the scholarship case at an all-white prep school really fucked with your head, didn't it?

YAZ. I should've gone to Edison.

ELLIOT. Public school in *el barrio.* You wouldn't have survived there for a day.

YAZ. Half our cousins didn't survive there.

ELLIOT. True. But you would've pissed your pants. At least their pants was dry when they went down.

YAZ. I thought *Abuela* dying, that would be the end of us. But Ginny grabbed the torch. Christmas, Easter. Now what? Our family may be fucked up but we had somewhere to go. A kitchen that connected us. Plastic-covered sofas where we could park our communal asses.

ELLIOT. Pop's selling the house. And the plastic-covered sofas. He's moving back to the Bronx, be with his sisters.

YAZ. You going with him? *(Elliot shrugs.)* Wow. I mean, once that living room is gone. I may never step foot in North Philly again

ELLIOT. I could go out to L.A. and be a movie star.

YAZ. You need a manager? Shoot, I'm coming witchu. Forget Philly.

ELLIOT. Change of scene, baby. Dream team.

YAZ. Probably we should order some flowers first, though. Don'tcha think?

ELLIOT. Orchid Paradise? *(Yaz hands him the brochure. To the florist:)* Sir?

Scene 6

The chat room. Orangutan is online, seems upset.

ORANGUTAN. 2:38 A.M. Tuesday. The witching hour. *(Chutes&Ladders logs on.)*

CHUTES&LADDERS. 1:38 P.M. Monday. The lunch hour.

ORANGUTAN. I'm in a gay bar slash internet café in the city of Sapporo. Deafening dance music.

CHUTES&LADDERS. Sure you should be in a bar, little monkey?

ORANGUTAN. *(Disappointed.)* I flew halfway around the world and guess what? It was still me who got off the plane. *(Taking comfort.)* Sapporo is always open. The world turns upside down at night.

CHUTES&LADDERS. You're in a city named after a beer sitting in a bar. Go home.

ORANGUTAN. Everything in this country makes sense but me. The noodles in soup make sense. The woodpecker outside my window every evening? Completely logical. The girls getting out of school in their miniskirts and shy smiles? Perfectly natural. I'm floating. I'm a cloud. My existence is one sustained out-of-body experience. It doesn't matter if I change my shoes, there's not a pair I've ever been able to fill. I'm a baby in a basket on an endless river. Wherever I go, I don't make sense there.

CHUTES&LADDERS. Hey little monkey. How many days you got?

ORANGUTAN. I think day ninety-six is when the demons really come out to play.

CHUTES&LADDERS. Ninety-six? Girl, hang your hat on that.

ORANGUTAN. I really really really want to smoke crack.

CHUTES&LADDERS. Yeah, well, don't.

ORANGUTAN. Distract me from myself. What do you really really really want, Chutes&Ladders?

CHUTES&LADDERS. I wouldn't say no to a new car — my Tercel is one sorry sight.

ORANGUTAN. What else?

CHUTES&LADDERS. Tuesday's crossword. On Monday I'm done by the time I sit at my desk. I wish every day could be a Tuesday.

ORANGUTAN. What about your son? Don't you really really really want to call him?

CHUTES&LADDERS. By all accounts, having me be a stranger these ten years has given him the best decade of his life.

ORANGUTAN. I've known you for how long?

CHUTES&LADDERS. Three Christmas Eves. When you logged on, you were a stone cold user. We sang Christmas carols online all night. Now you've got ninety days.

ORANGUTAN. Can I ask you a personal question? What's your day job?

CHUTES&LADDERS. IRS. GS4 paper pusher.

ORANGUTAN. Got any vacation days?

CHUTES&LADDERS. A solid collection. I haven't taken a vacation in ten years.

ORANGUTAN. Do you have money?

CHUTES&LADDERS. Enough to eat steak on Friday nights. Enough to buy pay-per-view boxing.

ORANGUTAN. Yeah, I bet that's all the pay per view you buy. *(Pause.)* Enough money to fly to Japan? *(Pause.)*

CHUTES&LADDERS. You should know I'm fifty years old on a good day, I eat three and a half donuts for breakfast and save the

27

remaining half for brunch, I have small hands, six toes on my left foot, and my face resembles a corgi.

ORANGUTAN. If I was looking for a hot screw I wouldn't be logging onto this site.

CHUTES&LADDERS. Damn, was it something I said?

ORANGUTAN. *(With honest admiration.)* I've been on this planet for thirty-one years and you're the only person I've ever met who's more sarcastic than I am yet still believes in God.

CHUTES&LADDERS. *(Taking the compliment.)* Says the agnostic.

ORANGUTAN. The atheist. Who is very envious of believers. My brain is my biggest enemy — always arguing my soul into a corner. *(Pause.)* I like you. Come to Japan. We can go get an ice cream. I can show you the countryside.

CHUTES&LADDERS. I don't have a passport. If my Tercel can't drive there, I generally don't go.

ORANGUTAN. Come save me in Japan. Be my knight in shining armor.

CHUTES&LADDERS. I'll admit, I'm a dashing concept. If you saw my flesh and blood, you'd be disappointed.

ORANGUTAN. I see my flesh and blood every day and I've learned to live with the disappointment.

CHUTES&LADDERS. I'm the squarest of the square. I live in a square house on a square block watching a square box eating square-cut fries.

ORANGUTAN. I get it. You were the kid who colored inside the lines.

CHUTES&LADDERS. No, I was the kid who ate the crayons. Was. I went clean and all personality left my life. Flew right out the window. I had to take life on life's terms. Messy, disappointing, bad shit happens to good people, coffee stains on my necktie, boring life.

ORANGUTAN. Maybe we could hang out and have a relationship that has very little to do with crack or addiction or history. We could watch DVDs and microwave popcorn and take walks on the waterfront while we gossip about celebrities. It could be the land of the living.

CHUTES&LADDERS. Stay in the box. Keep things in their place. It's a simple, effective recipe for ten clean years.

ORANGUTAN. Forget simple. I want a goddamn challenge.

CHUTES&LADDERS. You're in recovery and work in a foreign country. That's a challenge.

ORANGUTAN. No. No, it's fucking not. Not if I just stay anonymous and alone. Like every day of my shit life so far. A friend, the kind that is nice to you and you are nice to in return. That would push the comfort zone. The invitation is open. Come tear my shyness open.

CHUTES&LADDERS. Alright, now you're being weird. Can we change the subject? *(Haikumom appears. She's reading the newspaper.)*

HAIKUMOM. Orangutan, cover your ears.

ORANGUTAN. Big Brother, always watching.

HAIKUMOM. Cover your ears, kiddo.

ORANGUTAN. That doesn't really work online.

HAIKUMOM. Okay, Chutes&Ladders, can we G-Chat? One on one?

ORANGUTAN. Come on! No talking behind backs.

HAIKUMOM. Fine. Chutes&Ladders, you listening?

CHUTES&LADDERS. Lord have mercy, spit it out.

HAIKUMOM. Orangutan may be immature …

ORANGUTAN. Hey.

HAIKUMOM. She may be annoying at times …

ORANGUTAN. What the f?

HAIKUMOM. She may be overbearing and self-obsessed and a little bit of a concern troll and she can type faster than she can think which often leads to diarrhea of the keyboard —

CHUTES&LADDERS. Your point?

HAIKUMOM. But she's telling you, "Be my friend." When's the last time someone opened your closet door, saw all them skeletons, and said, "Wassup?! Can I join the party?"

CHUTES&LADDERS. Alright, my wrist is officially slapped. Thank you, oh nagging wives.

HAIKUMOM. Internal Revenue Service, 300 North Los Angeles Street, 90012? Is that you?

CHUTES&LADDERS. Need my name, too? It's Wilkie. I'll leave it at that.

HAIKUMOM. I'm sending you a care package. Orangutan, you can uncover your ears now. I love you.

ORANGUTAN. Middle finger. *(Fountainhead's logon appears.)*

FOUNTAINHEAD. Hey all, thanks for the warm two-by-four to my head.

HAIKUMOM. Alright, look who's back.

FOUNTAINHEAD. Knives sharpened? Last night we ran out of butter while my wife was cooking and she sent me to the store and it took every bit of strength I could summon not to make a "wrong turn" to that parking lot I know so well. I got the butter and on the car ride home, I couldn't help it, I drove by the lot, and there was my dealer in the shadows. My brain went on attack. "Use one more time just to prove you won't need another hit tomorrow." I managed to keep on driving and bring the butter home. Major victory. And my wife pulls it out of the plastic bag and says, "This is unsalted. I said salted." Then she feels guilty so she says never mind, never mind, she'll just add a little extra salt to the pie crust but I insist. "No, no, no, my wife deserves the right kind of butter and she's gonna get it!" I mean, I bark it, I'm already halfway out the door, my heart was racing all the way to the parking lot and raced even harder when I sat in the car and smoked. So, Michael Jordan is benched with a broken foot. But he'll come back in the finals.

HAIKUMOM. Thanks for the update, Fountainhead. You may not believe this, but we were missing you and worried about you. Don't beat yourself up about the slip. You had three days clean. This time you'll make it to day four.

FOUNTAINHEAD. Be ambitious. Why not reach for a whopping five?

ORANGUTAN. Maybe you'll make it to day thirty if you tell your wife.

FOUNTAINHEAD. I told you, I have my reasons, I cannot do that. My wife has some emotional issues.

ORANGUTAN. *(Sarcastic.)* No!

FOUNTAINHEAD. Listen? Please? Are you capable of that? She's in therapy twice a week. Depression, manic. I don't want to be the reason she goes down a tailspin. I actually have her best interests in mind.

CHUTES&LADDERS. Yawn.

FOUNTAINHEAD. Ah, Chutes&Ladders. I could feel you circling like a vulture. Weigh in, by all means.

CHUTES&LADDERS. And I repeat. Yawn.

FOUNTAINHEAD. Chutes&Ladders, why do I get the feeling you'd be the first in line for tickets to watch me smoke again? That you'd be in the bleachers cheering if I relapse?

CHUTES&LADDERS. How can you relapse when you don't even think you're addicted?

FOUNTAINHEAD. If you read my original post clearly, I wrote that it's a psychological addiction, not like heroin.

CHUTES&LADDERS. Well, see then, you're not a junkie after all.

FOUNTAINHEAD. What is this, first-grade recess?

CHUTES&LADDERS. No, this is a site for crackheads trying not to be crackheads anymore. If you're not a crackhead, leave, we don't want you, you are irrelevant, get off my lawn, go.

HAIKUMOM. Chutes&Ladders, please.

CHUTES&LADDERS. I got this.

ORANGUTAN. He's still logged on.

CHUTES&LADDERS. Hey Fountainhead, why did you come to this website?

FOUNTAINHEAD. Because I thoroughly enjoy getting shit on.

HAIKUMOM. Censored.

CHUTES&LADDERS. Why do you want to be here?

FOUNTAINHEAD. Want? The two times I've logged on here I've wanted to vomit.

CHUTES&LADDERS. Well? Did you receive some sort of invitation? Did one of us ask you here?

FOUNTAINHEAD. Look, I'm the first to say it. I have a problem.

CHUTES&LADDERS. Adam had problems. Eve had problems. Why are you here?

FOUNTAINHEAD. To get information.

CHUTES&LADDERS. Go to Wikipedia. Why are you here?

FOUNTAINHEAD. Because I smoke crack.

CHUTES&LADDERS. Go to a dealer. Why are you here?

FOUNTAINHEAD. Because I plan to stop smoking crack.

CHUTES&LADDERS. Fine, when your son has a tummy ache in the middle of the night and walks in on you tweaking and geeking just tell him, "Don't worry, Junior, Daddy's sucking on a glass dick — "

HAIKUMOM. *(Overlaps.)* Hey!

CHUTES&LADDERS. " — But Daddy makes 300K and this is all a part of Daddy's plan!"

FOUNTAINHEAD. I'M A FUCKING CRACKHEAD.

HAIKUMOM. *(Apologetic.)* Censored.

FOUNTAINHEAD. Fuck you, Chutes&Ladders.

HAIKUMOM. Bleep.

FOUNTAINHEAD. Fuck you … Don't talk about my sons. Don't fucking talk about my boys.

HAIKUMOM. Bleep again.

FOUNTAINHEAD. Are you happy, Chutes&Ladders?

CHUTES&LADDERS. Absolutely not, my friend. I'm a crack-head too and I wouldn't wish it on my worst enemy.

FOUNTAINHEAD. And I made 300K, I'm currently unemployed. An unemployed crackhead. At least I still have all my teeth. *(They laugh.)* Better than I can say for my dealer.

CHUTES&LADDERS. *(Being a friend.)* Ex-dealer, man.

FOUNTAINHEAD. Ex-dealer. Thank you.

HAIKUMOM. Fountainhead, welcome to the dinner party. Granted, it's a party we never wanted to be invited to, but pull up a chair and pass the salt. Some people here may pour it in your wounds. Just like you, we've all crawled on the floor with a flash-light. We've thrown out the Brillo and bought some more. But guess what? You had three days. For three days straight, you didn't try to kill yourself on an hourly basis. Please. Talk to your wife about your addiction. You need every supporting resource. You are in for the fight of your life. You mentioned Wharton. I live in Philly. If you're still in the area and you have an emergency or even a craving, email me directly. Any time of night. Don't take it lightly when I say a sober day for you is a sober day for me. I know you can do this but I know you can't do it alone. So stop being a highly functioning isolator and start being a highly dysfunctional person. The only way out it is through it.

ORANGUTAN. *(Nostalgic.)* Slogans …

HAIKUMOM. Y'all know I know 'em all.

CHUTES&LADDERS. They saved my life.

ORANGUTAN. Your personal favorite. Go.

HAIKUMOM. "Nothing changes if nothing changes." *(Elliot appears at the boxing gym, punching a bag. The Ghost watches him.)*

GHOST. *Momken men-fadluck ted-dini gawaz saffari?*

ORANGUTAN. "It came to pass, it didn't come to stay."

FOUNTAINHEAD. "I obsessively pursue feeling good, no matter how bad it makes me feel."

CHUTES&LADDERS. Okay, now!

ORANGUTAN. Nice!

HAIKUMOM. Rookie don't play!

GHOST. *Momken men-fadluck ted-dini gawaz saffari? (Yaz appears with a pen and notepad, writing.)*

YAZ. "We are gathered here in remembrance."

ORANGUTAN. "One hit is too many, one thousand never enough."

HAIKUMOM. "Have an at-ti-tude of gra-ti-tude."

CHUTES&LADDERS. "If you are eating a shit sandwich, chances are you ordered it."

ORANGUTAN. Ding ding ding. We have a winner!

HAIKUMOM. Censored. But good one.

YAZ. *(Crossing out, scribbling.)* "Today we send off our beloved Ginny P. Ortiz."

GHOST. *Momken men-fadluck ted-dini gawaz saffari?*

HAIKUMOM. *(Turning a page in the paper.)* Oh shit!

ORANGUTAN. CENSORED! YES! Whooooooo!

HAIKUMOM. You got me.

ORANGUTAN. *(Victorious.)* You know how long I've been waiting to do that?!

HAIKUMOM. My sister Ginny's in the *Daily News*! A nice big picture!

GHOST. *Momken men-fadluck ted-dini gawaz saffari?*

YAZ. *(Scribbling, erasing..)* "Ginny P. Ortiz was known to many as Mami Ginny."

HAIKUMOM. "Eugenia P. Ortiz, A Force For Good In Philadelphia!" That's my sister all right! Page 46 ... *(Haikumom looks for the page. Elliot punches harder. His leg is starting to bother him.)*

ELLIOT. Your leg feels great. Your leg feels like a million bucks. No pain. No pain.

HAIKUMOM. *(Finding the page.)* Obituaries? "In lieu of flowers contributions may be made to ..." *(Haikumom drops the newspaper. The Ghost blows on Elliot, knocking him to the floor. Intermission.)*

Scene 7

A diner. Odessa and John, a.k.a. Fountainhead, sit in a booth.

ODESSA. To lapsed Catholics. *(They clink coffee mugs.)* And you thought we had nothing in common.

JOHN. When did you become interested in Buddhism?

ODESSA. My older brother used to terrorize me during Mass. He would point to a statue, tell me about the evil spirit hiding behind it. Fangs, claws. I thought Saint Lazarus was gonna come to life and suck my eyes out. Buddhism? Not scary. If there's spirits, they're hiding inside you.

JOHN. Aren't those the scariest kind?

ODESSA. So, how many days do you have? It should be two now.

JOHN. I put my son's picture on my cell phone so if I get the urge, I can just look at him instead.

ODESSA. How many days?

JOHN. *(Small talk.)* I love Puerto Rico. On my honeymoon we stayed at that hotel in Old San Juan, the old convent. *(Odessa shrugs.)* And that Spanish fort at the top of the city? El Morro?

ODESSA. I've always been meaning to make it there.

JOHN. There are these keyholes where the cannons used to fit, and the view of the waves through them, you can practically see the Spanish Armada approaching.

ODESSA. I mean, one of these days I've gotta make it to P.R.

JOHN. Oh. I just figured …

ODESSA. The Jersey shore. Atlantic City. The Philadelphia airport. Oh, I've been places.

JOHN. On an actual plane?

ODESSA. I only fly first class, and I'm still saving for that ticket. *(Odessa's cell phone rings.)*

JOHN. You're a popular lady.

ODESSA. *(Into her phone, her demeanor completely changing.)* What? I told you, the diner on Spring Garden and Third. I'm busy, come in an hour. One hour. Now stop calling me and asking fucking directions. *(She hangs up.)*

JOHN. Says the one who censors.

ODESSA. My sister died.

JOHN. Right. You sure you're okay?

ODESSA. She's dead, ain't nothing left to do. People act like the world is going to fall apart.

JOHN. You write very Zen messages. And yet.

ODESSA. My family knows every button to push.

JOHN. My condolences. *(Pause.)* You don't strike me as a computer nerd. I used to employ an entire floor of them.

ODESSA. You should've seen me at first, pecking with two fingers. Now I'm like an octopus with ten little tentacles. In my neck of the woods, staying clean is like trying to tap dance on a mine-field. The website fills the hours. So how are we gonna fill yours, huh? When was the last time you picked up a javelin?

JOHN. Senior year of high school.

ODESSA. *(Hands him a sheet of paper.)* There's a sober softball league. Fairmount Park, games on Sundays. Sober bowling on Thursdays.

JOHN. I lied in my first post. I've been smoking crack for two years. I've tried quitting hundreds of times. Day two? Please, I'm in the seven hundredth day of hell.

ODESSA. You got it out of your system. Most people lie at one time or another on the site. The good news is, two years in, there's still time. *(Hands him another sheet of paper.)* Talbot Recovery Center in Atlanta. It's designed for professionals with addictions. Paradise Recovery in Hawaii. They actually check your income before admitting you. Just for the wealthy. This place in Jersey, it's right over the bridge, they have an outpatient program for professionals like you.

JOHN. I'm tenacious. I'm driven. I love my parents.

ODESSA. Pitchforks against tanks.

JOHN. I relish in paying my taxes.

ODESSA. And you could be dead tomorrow. *(Pause.)* Is your dealer male or female?

JOHN. I had a few. Flushed their numbers down the toilet like you suggested.

ODESSA. Your original connection. The one who got you hooked.

JOHN. Female.

ODESSA. Did you have sex with her?

JOHN. You don't beat around the bush, do you?

ODESSA. I'll take that as a yes. *(No answer.)* Do you prefer sex when you're high to sex when you're sober?

JOHN. I've never really analyzed it.

ODESSA. It can be a dangerous cocktail. Some men get off on smoking and fucking.

JOHN. All men get off on fucking.

ODESSA. Are you scared your wife will find out you're addicted to crack? Or are you scared she'll find out what came of your wedding vows?

JOHN. I should go.

ODESSA. We just ordered.

JOHN. I promised my son. There's a science fair tomorrow. Something about dioramas and Krazy Glue.

35

ODESSA. Don't talk about them. Get sober for them.

JOHN. Fuck you.

ODESSA. Leave me three bucks for your coffee. *(He pulls out three dollars. She throws the money back at him.)* You picked up the phone and called me.

JOHN. *(He sits down again.)* I don't know how to do this. I've never done this before.

ODESSA. I have and it usually doesn't end up so good. One in twenty, maybe, hang around. Most people just don't write one day and then thirty days and then you're wondering … And sometimes you get the answer. 'Cuz their wife looks on their computer and sees the website and logs on and writes, "I found him face-down in the snow."

JOHN. How many day ones did you have?

ODESSA. Seven years' worth.

JOHN. Do you still crave?

ODESSA. On the good days, only every hour. Would you rather be honest with your wife, or would you rather end up like me? *(Pause.)* That wasn't rhetorical.

JOHN. You're not exactly what I wanted to be when I grew up.

ODESSA. Truth. Now we're talking. *(Elliot and Yaz enter.)*

YAZ. There she is. *(Elliot and Yaz sit down in the booth.)*

ELLIOT. You were supposed to meet us at the flower place.

YAZ. The deposit was due at nine.

ODESSA. My alarm clock didn't go off.

ELLIOT. Were you up on that chat room all night?

ODESSA. *(Ignoring him.)* Can I get a refill, please?

ELLIOT. Where's the money?

ODESSA. I told you I don't have any money.

ELLIOT. And you think I do? I been paying for Mami Ginny's meds for six months straight —

ODESSA. Well, get it from Yaz's mom.

YAZ. My mom put in for the headstone. She got an expensive one.

ODESSA. Headstone? She's getting cremated.

YAZ. She still needs a proper Catholic piece of granite. Right beside *Abuela*, right beside your dad and sister and brother.

ELLIOT. And daughter.

YAZ. Everyone agreed.

ODESSA. No one asked my opinion.

ELLIOT. Everyone who showed up to the family meeting.

ODESSA. I wasn't invited.

YAZ. I texted you twice.

ODESSA. I was out of minutes.

ELLIOT. We just spoke on the phone.

ODESSA. Whatchu want me to do, Elliot, if I say I ain't got no fucking money, I ain't got no money.

JOHN. Hi, I'm John, nice to meet you.

YAZ. Yazmin.

ELLIOT. You one of mom's rehab buddies?

JOHN. We know each other from work.

ELLIOT. You scrub toilets?

ODESSA. *(To John.)* I'm a practitioner of the custodial arts.

ELLIOT. Is she your sponsor?

JOHN. *(To Odessa.)* I thought this was going to be a private meeting.

ELLIOT. I'm her son.

JOHN. *(To Odessa.)* You must have been young.

ELLIOT. But I was raised by my Aunt Ginny and that particular aunt just died. *(To Odessa.)* So now, you got three hours to find some money to pay for one basket of flowers in her funeral.

YAZ. We're all supposed to be helping out.

ODESSA. You both know I run out of minutes all the time. No one could be bothered to drive by and tell me face to face?

ELLIOT. Because you always bothered to drive by and say hello to Mami Ginny when you knew she was sick? Because you bothered to hit me up one time this week and say, "Elliot, I'm sorry your mom died."

ODESSA. You still got one mom alive.

ELLIOT. Really? You want to go there?

YAZ. The flower place needs the money today.

ODESSA. She was my sister and you are my son, too.

YAZ. Guys. Two hundred dollars by end of business day.

ODESSA. That's my rent.

ELLIOT. Then fifty.

ODESSA. I just spent fifty getting my phone back on.

ELLIOT. Ten dollars. For the woman who raised your son! Do we hear ten dollars? Going once!

ODESSA. I spent my last ten at the post office.

ELLIOT. Going twice! *(John goes into his wallet.)*

JOHN. Here's fifty. *(They all look at him like he's crazy. He pulls out some more money.)* Two hundred? *(Elliot pushes the money back to John with one pointer finger, like the bills might be contaminated.)*

37

ELLIOT. No offense, I don't take money from users.

JOHN. I'm not … I think that was my cue.

ODESSA. Sit down. My son was just going.

ELLIOT. Did world's best Mom here tell you about her daughter?

ODESSA. I'm about to throw this coffee in your fucking face.

YAZ. Come on, Elliot, I'll pay for the flowers. *(Elliot doesn't get up.)*

ELLIOT. I looked at that chat room once. The woman I saw there? She's literally not the same person I know. *(To John.)* Did she tell you how she became such a saint?

JOHN. We all have skeletons.

ELLIOT. Yeah well, she's an archaeological dig. Did she tell you about her daughter?

ODESSA. *(Suddenly resigned.)* Go ahead, I ain't got no secrets.

YAZ. *(Getting up.)* Excuse me.

ELLIOT. Sit here and listen, Yaz. You were born with a silver spoon and you can't stand how it was for me.

YAZ. I said I'd pay for the goddamn flowers so LET'S GO. NOW!

ELLIOT. My sister and I had the stomach flu, right? For a whole day we couldn't keep nothing down.

ODESSA. Three days … You were vomiting three days straight.

ELLIOT. Medicine, juice, anything we ate, it would come right back up. Your coworker here took us to Children's Hospital.

ODESSA. Jefferson.

ELLIOT. It was wall to wall packed. Every kid in Philly had this bug. E.R.'s were turning kids away. They gave us a flier about stomach flu and sent us home. Bright blue paper. Little cartoon diagrams. It said give your kids a spoonful of water every five minutes.

ODESSA. A teaspoon.

ELLIOT. A small enough amount that they can keep it down. Five minutes. Spoon. Five minutes. Spoon. I remember thinking, wow, this is it. Family time. Quality time. Just the three of us. Because it was gentle, the way you said, "Open up." I opened my mouth, you put that little spoon of water into my mouth. That little bit of relief. And then I watched you do the same thing with my little sister. And I remember being like, "Wow, I love you, Mom. My moms is alright." Five minutes. Spoon. Five minutes. Spoon. But you couldn't stick to something simple like that. You couldn't sit still like that. You had to have your thing. That's where I stop remembering.

ODESSA. I left.

ELLIOT. A Department of Human Services report. That's my memory. Six hours later a neighbor kicks in the door. Me and my sister are lying in a pile of laundry. My shorts was all messed up. And what I really don't remember is my sister. Quote. Female infant, approximately two years, pamper and tear ducts dry, likely cause of death, dehydration. 'Cuz when you dehydrate you can't form a single tear.

JOHN. *(To Elliot.)* I'm very sorry … *(He puts some money on the table.)* For the coffee. *(Exits.)*

ELLIOT. That's some friend you got there. *(Pause.)*

YAZ. Mary Lou. We never say her name out loud. Mary Lou. Mary Lou. *(To Odessa.)* One time you came to babysit me, you brought Elliot and Mary Lou—she had just learned to use a straw and she had this soda from 7-Eleven. She didn't want to give me a sip. You yelled at her so bad, you totally cursed her out and I said, "You're not supposed to yell at people like that!" And you said, "No, Yaz, she's gotta learn that y'all are cousins, y'all are flesh and blood, and we share everything. In this family we share *everything.*" You walked out of the room, came back from the kitchen with four straws, sat us down on the floor in a circle, pointed to me and said, "You first." I took a sip. "Elliot's turn." He sipped. "Mary Lou's turn." She sipped. Then you sipped. You made us do like that, taking turns, going around the circle, til that cup was empty. *(Odessa hands Elliot a key.)*

ODESSA. The pawn shop closes at five. Go into my house. Take my computer. Pawn it. However much you get, put it towards a few flowers, okay? *(Odessa exits.)*

Scene 8

Split scene. Odessa's living room and the chat room. Chutes&Ladders holds a phone.

ORANGUTAN. Did you hit the call button yet?

CHUTES&LADDERS. I'm working on it.

ORANGUTAN. Where are you? Are you at home?

CHUTES&LADDERS. *Jeopardy's* on mute.

ORANGUTAN. Dude, turn off the tube. This is serious. Did you even dial?

CHUTES&LADDERS. Yeah, yeah. *(He does.)* Alright, it's ringing. What am I going to say?

ORANGUTAN. "Hi, son, it's Dad."

CHUTES&LADDERS. Wendell. That's his name. *(Hangs up.)* No answer.

ORANGUTAN. As in, you hung up?

CHUTES&LADDERS. Yes. I hung up.

ORANGUTAN. Dude, way too quick!

CHUTES&LADDERS. What do you have, a stopwatch? Do you know the average time before someone answers a telephone?

ORANGUTAN. Three point two rings.

CHUTES&LADDERS. According to …

ORANGUTAN. I don't reveal my sources.

CHUTES&LADDERS. Look, my son's a grown man with a good life.

ORANGUTAN. Quit moping and dial Wendell's number.

CHUTES&LADDERS. This Japan thing is cramping my style. Different networks, different time zones. No concurrent *Jeopardy* watching.

ORANGUTAN. Deflection: nostalgia.

CHUTES&LADDERS. Humor me.

ORANGUTAN. *(Humoring him.)* How's my little Trebeky doing?

CHUTES&LADDERS. He's had work done. Man looks younger than he did twenty years ago.

ORANGUTAN. Needle or knife?

CHUTES&LADDERS. Needle. His eyes are still in the right place.

ORANGUTAN. Well, it's working. Meow. Purrrrr. Any good categories?

CHUTES&LADDERS. Before and After.

ORANGUTAN. I love Before and After! But I'll go with … Quit Stalling for two hundred. *(She hums a bit of the* Jeopardy *theme.)*

CHUTES&LADDERS. It's ringing.

ORANGUTAN. My stopwatch is running.

CHUTES&LADDERS. Still ringing.

ORANGUTAN. You're going to be great.

CHUTES&LADDERS. It rang again.

ORANGUTAN. You're a brave soul. *(We hear a man's voice at the other end of the line say, "Hello?" Chutes&Ladders hangs up.)*

CHUTES&LADDERS. He must not be around.

ORANGUTAN. Leave a voicemail.

CHUTES&LADDERS. Maybe next time. *(Chutes&Ladders logs off.)*
ORANGUTAN. Hey! Don't log off, come on. Chutes&Ladders.
Whatever happened to tough love? Log back on, we'll do a cross-
word. You can't fly before Final Jeopardy! Sigh. Anyone else online?
Haikumom? I'm still waiting for that daily poem ... Bueller?
Bueller? *(In Odessa's living room, Elliot and Yaz enter.)*
YAZ. Wow, look at that computer. Stone age.
ELLIOT. Fred Flinstone shit.
YAZ. Positively *Doctor Who.*
ELLIOT. *Doctor Who?*
YAZ. That computer is actually worse than what they give the
adjuncts at Swarthmore.
ELLIOT. What does "adjunct" even mean?
YAZ. Exactly. It's the nicest thing she owns.
ELLIOT. Let's not act like this is some heroic sacrifice. Like this
makes her the world's martyr.
YAZ. We're not going to get more than fifteen bucks for it.
ELLIOT. Symbols matter, Yaz. This isn't about the money. This is
shaking hands. This is tipping your hat. This is holding the door
open. This is the bare minimum, the least effort possible to earn
the label "person." *(Looks at the screen.)* What do you think her
password is? *(Types.)* "Odessa." Nope. "Odessaortiz." Nope.
YAZ. It's probably Elliot. *(He types. Haikumom's log-on appears.)*
ELLIOT. The irony.
YAZ. I think legally that might be like breaking and entering.
ELLIOT. *(Typing.)* Hello? Oh shit, it posted.
ORANGUTAN. Haikumom! Hit me with those seventeen sylla-
bles, baby!
YAZ. Haikumom? What the hell is that?
ELLIOT. Her username. She has the whole world thinking she's
some Chinese prophet.
YAZ. Haiku are Japanese.
ELLIOT. "Haiku are Japanese." *(Typing.)* Hello, Orangutan. How
are you?
ORANGUTAN. *(Formal.)* I am fine. How are you?
ELLIOT. *(Typing.)* So, I guess you like monkeys, huh?
ORANGUTAN. An orangutan is a primate.
YAZ. Elliot.
ELLIOT. Chill.
ORANGUTAN. And this primate has ninety-eight days. That

41

deserves a poem, don't you think?

ELLIOT. *(Typing.)* I don't have a poem, but I have a question. What does crack feel like?

ORANGUTAN. What?

YAZ. Elliot, cut it out.

ELLIOT. *(Typing.)* Sometimes I'm amazed I don't know firsthand.

ORANGUTAN. Who is this?

ELLIOT. *(Typing.)* How does it make your brain feel?

ORANGUTAN. Like it's flooded with dopamine. Listen, cyberstalker, if you came here for shits and giggles, we are a sadly unfunny bunch.

ELLIOT. *(Typing.)* Are you just a smoker or do you inject it right into your eyeballs?

ORANGUTAN. Who the fuck is this?

ELLIOT. *(Typing.)* Haikumom.

ORANGUTAN. Bullshit, you didn't censor me. Quit screwing around, hacker, who are you?

YAZ. You think Ginny would want you acting this way?

ELLIOT. I think Mami Ginny would want Mami Odessa to pay for a single flower on her fucking casket.

YAZ. *(Types.)* This is not Haikumom. It's her son.

ORANGUTAN. Well, if you're looking for the friends and family thread, you have to go to the home page and create a new logon. This particular forum is for people actually in recovery. Wait, her son the actor? From the Crest ad?

ELLIOT. *(Typing.)* Colgate.

ORANGUTAN. "*Sonrisa* baby!" I saw that on YouTube! Your teeth are insanely white. Ever worked in Hollywood?

ELLIOT. *(Typing.)* Psh. I just had this guy begging me to do a feature film. Gritty, documentary-style, about Marines in Iraq. I just don't want to do anything cheesy.

ORANGUTAN. So you're the war hero …

ELLIOT. *(Typing.)* Haikumom brags.

ORANGUTAN. How's your recovery going? *(No answer.)* This is the crack forum, but there's a really good pain-meds forum on this site, too. Link here.

YAZ. What is she talking about?

ORANGUTAN. There's a few war vets on that forum, just like you. You'd be in good company.

YAZ. Pain meds? Elliot? *(He doesn't respond. Yaz types.)* What are you talking about?

ORANGUTAN. Haikumom told us about your history.

YAZ. *(Typing.)* What history?

ORANGUTAN. Sorry. Maybe she told us in confidence.

ELLIOT. Confidence? They call this shit "worldwide" for a reason.

YAZ. *(Typing.)* I can search all the threads right now.

ORANGUTAN. That you had a bunch of leg surgeries in Iraq. That if a soldier said they hurt, the docs practically threw pills at them. That you OD'd three times and were in the hospital for it. She was real messed up about it. I guess she had hoped the fruit would fall a little farther from the tree.

YAZ. *(To Elliot.)* Is this true?

ELLIOT. I wasn't a soldier. I was a Marine. Soldiers is the army.

YAZ. Oh my god.

ELLIOT. *(Takes the keyboard, types.)* What I am: sober. What I am not and never will be: a pathetic junkie like you. *(He unplugs the computer. He throws the keyboard on the ground. He starts unplugging cables violently.)*

YAZ. Hold on. Just stop it, Elliot! Stop it!

ELLIOT. The one time I ever reached out to her for anything and she made me a story on a website.

YAZ. Why wouldn't you ask me for help? Why would you deal with that alone?

ELLIOT. The opposite of alone. I seen barracks that looked like dope houses. It was four months in my life, it's over. We've chopped up a lot of shit together, Yaz, but we ain't gonna chop this up. This shit stays in the vault. You got me?

YAZ. No!

ELLIOT. Yaz. *(He looks her straight in the eye.)* Please. Please.

YAZ. I want to grab the sky and smash it into pieces. Are you clean?

ELLIOT. The only thing I got left from those days is the nightmares. That's when he came, and some days I swear he ain't never gonna leave.

YAZ. Who? *(Elliot tries to walk away from the conversation, but The Ghost is there, blocking his path.)* Who?!

ELLIOT. *(Almost like a child.)* Please, Yaz. Please end this conversation. Don't make me beg, Yaz.

YAZ. The pawn shop closes in fifteen minutes. I'll get the monitor, you grab the computer.

Scene 9

Chutes&Ladders is at work, on his desk phone. A bundled pile of mail is on his desk. He takes off the rubber band, browses. Junk, mostly.

CHUTES&LADDERS. *(Into the work phone.)* That's right. Three W's. Dot. Not the word, the punctuation mark. I-R-S. Not F like flamingo, S like Sam. Dot. Yup, another one. Gov. Grover orange victor. *(Orangutan appears, online.)*

ORANGUTAN. I'm doing it. I'm almost there. And I can chat! Japan is so advanced. Internet cafés are like parking meters here.

CHUTES&LADDERS. Where are you and what are you doing?

ORANGUTAN. Sapporo train station. Just did some research. Get this: In the early '80s, they straightened all the rivers in Hokkaido.

CHUTES&LADDERS. Why?

ORANGUTAN. To create jobs, the government straightened the rivers! Huge bodies of water, manual laborers, scientists, engineers, bulldozers, and the rivers became straight! How nuts is that?

CHUTES&LADDERS. People can't leave good enough alone. Why are humans so damn restless?

ORANGUTAN. It's not restlessness. It's ego. Massive, bizarre ego.

CHUTES&LADDERS. Can't let a river be a river. *(Into the phone.)* The forms link is on the left.

ORANGUTAN. Now it's the aughts, people keep being born, jobs still need creating, but there's no curves left to straighten, so, drum roll, the government is beginning a new program to put all the original turns back in the rivers! Ever heard of Kushiro?

CHUTES&LADDERS. Is that your new boyfriend's name?

ORANGUTAN. Ha. Ha ha ha. It's home of the hundred-mile-long Kushiro River, which is the pilot project, the first river they're trying to re-curve.

CHUTES&LADDERS. Kushiro River. Got it. Burned in the brain. One day I'll win a Trivial Pursuit wedge with that. *(Into the phone.)* You, too, ma'am. *(He hangs up.)*

ORANGUTAN. My train to Kushiro leaves in twenty minutes.

My heart is pounding.

CHUTES&LADDERS. I don't follow.

ORANGUTAN. Kushiro is the town where I was born. I'm going. I'm doing it.

CHUTES&LADDERS. Hold on, now you're throwing curveballs.

ORANGUTAN. In my hand is a sheet of paper. On the paper is the address of the house where my birth parents once lived. I'm going to knock on their door. *(Chutes&Ladder's desk phone rings.)*

CHUTES&LADDERS. *(Into the phone.)* Help desk, please hold. *(To Orangutan.)* How long have you had that address for?

ORANGUTAN. It's been burning a hole in my pocket for two days. I hounded my mom before I left Maine. She finally wrote down the name of the adoption agency. The first clue, the first evidence of who I was I ever had. I made a vow to myself, if I could stay sober for three months, I would track my parents down. So a few days ago class ended early, I went to the agency, showed my passport, and thirty minutes later I had an address on a piece of paper. Ask me anything about Kushiro. All I've done the last two days is research it. I'm an expert. Population, 190,000. There's a tech school, there's an airport.

CHUTES&LADDERS. Why are you telling me this? To get my blessing?

ORANGUTAN. I tell you about the things I do.

CHUTES&LADDERS. You don't want my opinion, you want my approval.

ORANGUTAN. Hand it over.

CHUTES&LADDERS. No.

ORANGUTAN. Don't get monosyllabic.

CHUTES&LADDERS. Take that piece of paper and use it as kindling for a warm winter fire.

ORANGUTAN. Jeez, what did they slip into your Wheaties this morning?

CHUTES&LADDERS. Do a ritual burning and never look back. You have three months. Do you know the worth in gold of three months? Don't give yourself a reason to go back to the shadows.

ORANGUTAN. I'm in recovery. I have no illusions about catharsis. I realize what will most likely happen is nothing. Maybe something tiny. A microscopic butterfly flapping her microscopic wings.

CHUTES&LADDERS. Live in the past, follow your ass.

ORANGUTAN. Don't you have the slightest ambition?

CHUTES&LADDERS. Yes, and I achieve it every day. Don't use and don't hurt anyone. Two things I used to do on a daily basis. I don't do them anymore. Done. Dream realized. No more dreaming. *(His phone rings again. Into the phone.)* Continue holding, please.

ORANGUTAN. When was the last time you went out on a limb?

CHUTES&LADDERS. Three odd weeks ago.

ORANGUTAN. Did you try Hazelnut instead of French Roast?

CHUTES&LADDERS. There's a new secretary down the hall, she's got a nice smile. I decided to go say hello. We had a little back and forth, I said, let's have lunch, she said maybe but meant no, I turned away, looked down and my tie was floating in my coffee cup.

ORANGUTAN. I waited three months to tell you this, every step of the way, the train ride, what the river looks like. What their front door looks like. *(Pause.)* I'm quitting this site. I hate this site. I fucking hate this site.

CHUTES&LADDERS. You're already losing it and you haven't even gotten on the train.

ORANGUTAN. Three days ago I suggested you and I meet face to face and you blew a fucking gasket.

CHUTES&LADDERS. That's what this is about?

ORANGUTAN. Don't flatter yourself. This is about me wanting relationships. With humans, not ones and zeroes. So we were once junkies. It's superficial. It's not real friendship.

CHUTES&LADDERS. I beg to differ.

ORANGUTAN. Prove me wrong.

CHUTES&LADDERS. Search down that address and a hundred bucks says your heart comes back a shattered light bulb.

ORANGUTAN. You mean, gasp, I'll actually FEEL something?

CHUTES&LADDERS. What are you going to do if the address is wrong? What if the building's been bulldozed? What if some new tenant lives there? What if the woman who gave you birth then gave you away answers the door?

ORANGUTAN. I DON'T KNOW! A concept you clearly avoid at all costs. Learn how to live, that's all I'm goddamn trying to do! *(His phone rings. He picks up the receiver and hangs it up.)*

CHUTES&LADDERS. I have three grandsons. You know how I know that? Because I rang my son's doorbell one day. Step 9, make amends. And his wife answered, and I don't blame her for hating me. But I saw three little boys in that living room and one of those

46

boys said, "Daddy, who's that man at the door?" And my son said to my grandson, "I don't know. He must be lost." My son came outside, closed the door behind him, exchanged a few cordial words and then asked me to go.

ORANGUTAN. So I shouldn't even try.

CHUTES&LADDERS. I had five years sober until that day.

ORANGUTAN. You really believe in your heart of hearts I should not even try. *(Pause.)* Coward. *(His phone rings. He unplugs the phone line.)*

CHUTES&LADDERS. You think it's easy being your friend?

ORANGUTAN. Sissy. You walk the goddamn earth scared of your own shadow, getting smaller and smaller, until you disappear.

CHUTES&LADDERS. You tease me. You insult me. It's like breathing to you.

ORANGUTAN. You fucking idiot. Why do little girls tease little boys on the playground at recess? Why the fuck were cooties invented? You fucking imbecile!

CHUTES&LADDERS. You disappeared for three months. I couldn't sleep for three months!

ORANGUTAN. I wanted to impress you. I wanted to log on and show you I could be better. And I was an idiot because you're just looking for cowards like you. I'm logging off. This is it. It's over.

CHUTES&LADDERS. Orangutan.

ORANGUTAN. Into the abyss I climb, looking for a flesh and blood hand to grasp onto.

CHUTES&LADDERS. Little monkey, stop it.

ORANGUTAN. I'm in the station. My train is in five minutes, you gave me all the motivational speech I need, I'm going to the platform, I'm getting on the train, I'm going to see the house where I was born. *(She logs off. Chutes&Ladders grabs his phone and hurls it into his wastebasket. He throws his calculator, his mail pile, his pen cup to the ground. Left on his desk is one padded envelope.)*

CHUTES&LADDERS. "To Chutes&Ladders Wilkie." "From Haikumom Ortiz." *(He rips it open, pulls out a deflated orange water wing, puts it over his hand.)*

47

Scene 10

Split scene. Lights rise on a church. Elliot and Yaz stand at the lectern.

YAZ. It is time to honor a woman.*

ELLIOT. A woman who built her community with a hammer and nails.

YAZ. A woman who knew her nation's history. Its African roots. European roots. Indigenous roots. A woman who refused to be enslaved but lived to serve.

ELLIOT. A carpenter, a nurse, a comedian, a cook.

YAZ. Eugenia Ortiz.

ELLIOT. Mami Ginny. *(Lights rise on Odessa's house. She sits on her floor. She scoops a spoonful of water from a mug, pours it onto the floor in a slow ribbon.)*

YAZ. She grew vegetables in her garden lot and left the gate open so anyone could walk in and pick dinner off the vine.

ELLIOT. She drank beer and told dirty jokes and even the never-crack-a-smile church ladies would be rolling laughing.

YAZ. She told me every time I visited, "Yaz, you're going to Juilliard."

ELLIOT. Every morning when I left for school, "Elliot, nobody can make you invisible but you." *(Lights rise on Sapporo train station. Orangutan is on the platform. We hear a loudspeaker boarding announcement in Japanese.)*

YAZ. Zero.

ELLIOT. Birth children.

YAZ. One.

ELLIOT. Adopted son. *(Odessa pours another spoonful of water on the floor. Again, it creates a slow ribbon.)*

YAZ. Three.

ELLIOT. Years in the Army Nurse Corps.

YAZ. Three.

---

* This eulogy is inspired by and owes much debt to Roger Zepernick's eulogy for Eugenia Burgos.

ELLIOT. Arrests for civil disobedience. I was in Iraq and she was demonstrating for peace.

YAZ. Forty seven.

ELLIOT. Wheelchair ramps she installed in homes with disabled children or elderly. *(Odessa pours another spoonful of water to the floor. A small pool is forming.)*

YAZ. Twelve.

ELLIOT. Abandoned lots she turned into city-recognized public gardens. *(Another spoonful.)*

YAZ. Twenty-two.

ELLIOT. Godchildren recognized by this church. *(Another spoonful.)*

YAZ. One hundred and thirty.

ELLIOT. Abandoned homes she refurbished and sold to young families. *(In the Sapporo station we hear a final loudspeaker boarding announcement. Orangutan is still on the platform. She seems frozen, like she cannot move.)*

YAZ. All while having a fresh pot of rice and beans on the stove every night. For any hungry stranger. And the pilgrims stopped. And they planted roots, because she was here. We are the living, breathing proof.

ELLIOT. I am the … Excuse me. *(He exits.)*

YAZ. Elliot is the standing, walking testimony to a life. She. Was. Here. *(Odessa turns the cup upside down. It is empty.)*

Scene 11

Chutes&Ladders at his desk. In front of him: an inflated orange water wing.

CHUTES&LADDERS. *(On the phone.)* Yeah, it's a 1995 Tercel. Midnight blue. It's got a few miles. A hundred and twenty thousand. But like I said, I'll give it to you for three hundred below Kelley Blue Book. Yup, automatic. Just got new brake pads. Cassette deck, mint condition. I'll even throw in a few tapes. Tina Turner and Lionel Richie. Oh, hold on, call waiting. *(He presses mute. Sings to himself.)*

A tisket, a tasket.
A green and yellow basket.
I bought a basket for my mommy.
On the way I dropped it.
Was it red? No no no no!
Was it brown? No no no no!
(Back into the phone.) Sorry about that. I got someone else interested. No, it's alright, I have them on hold. You need to see this thing tonight if you're serious. I put this listing up thirty minutes ago, my phone is ringing off the hook. Six-thirty? Hey, I didn't mention. Little lady has racing stripes.

Scene 12

Split scene. Lights rise on the Sapporo train station, same as before. Orangutan has laid down on the platform and fallen asleep, her backpack like a pillow.

Lights rise on Odessa's house, that night. Her phone rings. We hear loud knocking.

ELLIOT. *(Offstage.)* Mami Odessa! Open the door! *(More ringing. Offstage.)* Yo, Mom!

YAZ. *(Offstage.)* She's not there.

ELLIOT. *(Offstage.)* Can't you hear her phone ringing? Move out the way.

YAZ. *(Offstage.)* Be careful, your leg! *(A few kicks and the door bursts open. Yaz and Elliot enter, switch on the lights. Odessa is in a heap, motionless, on the floor. Yaz runs and holds Odessa in her arms.)* Oh shit. Odessa! Odessa! Wake up. *(She slaps her face a few times.)*

YAZ. Her pulse is racing. *(Yaz opens her cell phone, dials. Elliot finds a spoon on the floor.)*

ELLIOT. Oh no. Oh no you fucking didn't! MOM! Get up!

YAZ. *(Into the phone.)* Hi, I need an ambulance. I have someone unconscious here. I think it's an overdose, crack cocaine. Yes, she has a pulse. 33 Ontario Street. No, no seizures, she's just a lump,

what should we do while we wait? Okay. Yes. *(She hangs up.)*
They're on their way. Elevate her feet.

ELLIOT. Help me get her to the sofa. One, two, three. *(Elliot lifts her with Yaz's help. They struggle under her weight. In fact they lift the air. Odessa stands up, lucid, and watches the action: Elliot and Yaz struggling under her invisible weight.)*

YAZ. Watch her head.

ELLIOT. Aw, fuck, my leg.

YAZ. Careful. *(They set "Odessa" on the sofa, while Odessa watches, unseen, calm.)*

ODESSA. I must be in the terminal. Between flights. The layover.

YAZ. Oh god, not two in one day, please.

ELLIOT. She's been through this shit a million times. She's a survivor! WAKE UP! Call your mom. She'll get here before the ambulance. *(Yaz dials.)*

ODESSA. I've been to the airport, one time. My dad flew here from Puerto Rico. First time I met him. We stood by the baggage claim, his flight was late, we waited forever. There was one single, lone suitcase, spinning around a carousel.

YAZ. *(To Elliot.)* Voicemail. *(Into the phone.)* Mom? Call me back immediately, it's an emergency.

ELLIOT. Give me that. *(Grabs the phone.)* Titi, Odessa fucking OD'd and she's dying in her living room and I can't take this anymore! COME GET US before I walk off and leave her on the sofa! *(He hangs up.)*

YAZ. If you need to, go. No guilt. I got this.

ELLIOT. She's my mom. Can I be angry? Can you let me be angry?

YAZ. Why is this family plagued? *(Elliot gets up.)* Where are you going?

ELLIOT. To find something fragile. *(He exits. We hear something shatter.)*

ODESSA. Everyone had cleared away from the carousel. Everyone had their bags. But this one was unclaimed. It could still be there for all I know. Spiraling. Spinning. Looking for an owner. Abandoned. *(In the Sapporo station, a policeman enters with a bright, beaming flashlight and points it at Orangutan. In Odessa's house, a radiant white light suddenly pours in from above. Odessa looks up, is overwhelmed. It is beautiful. Yaz sees it.)*

YAZ. Dear god, do you see that?

ELLIOT. *(Enters, looks up, not seeing it.)* What?

51

YAZ. *(To Odessa.)* It's okay, Odessa, go, go, we love you, I love you *Titi,* you are good, you are good. Oh my god, she's beautiful.

ELLIOT. What are you talking about?

YAZ. It's okay, it's okay. We love you, Odessa.

POLICEMAN. *(In Japanese.)* Miss, miss, are you okay?

ORANGUTAN. *(Waking.)* English, please.

POLICEMAN. No sleeping on the floor.

ORANGUTAN. *(Getting up slowly.)* Sorry.

POLICEMAN. Are you sick?

ORANGUTAN. No.

POLICEMAN. Are you intoxicated?

ORANGUTAN. No. I'm very sorry. I just got tired. I'll go. I'm going.

POLICEMAN. Please, can I give you a hand?

ORANGUTAN. No. I got it. *(Orangutan exits. The policeman turns off his flashlight, exits. The sound of an ambulance siren and suddenly the white light disappears. Odessa crawls onto the couch and slips into Yaz's arms, where she's been all along.)*

YAZ. Holy shit …

ELLIOT. What's happening, Yaz? What the fuck was that?

YAZ. You've got to forgive her, Elliot. You have to.

Scene 13

The chat room.

CHUTES&LADDERS. Oh nagging wives? Orangutan? Hello? Earth to Orangutan. Come on, three days straight I been worrying about you. I have time-sensitive information. Ground control to Major Orangutan.

ORANGUTAN. Ta-da.

CHUTES&LADDERS. Where you been?

ORANGUTAN. Here. There. Morrisey and Nine Inch Nails on loop.

CHUTES&LADDERS. Is that what the kids like these days?

ORANGUTAN. *(Rolls eyes.)* That was me rolling my eyes.

CHUTES&LADDERS. Guess what I did.

ORANGUTAN. *(She shrugs.)* That was me shrugging.

CHUTES&LADDERS. Guess.

ORANGUTAN. Guess what I didn't do?

CHUTES&LADDERS. Meet your birth parents?

ORANGUTAN. Board the train.

CHUTES&LADDERS. Sorry.

ORANGUTAN. Don't apologize. You had my number.

CHUTES&LADDERS. Guess what I did.

ORANGUTAN. Told me so. Had my shit pegged.

CHUTES&LADDERS. I sold my Tercel. My plane lands in Narita Airport on Wednesday.

ORANGUTAN. What?

CHUTES&LADDERS. American Airlines flight 3312. Arriving 10:01 A.M.

ORANGUTAN. You're a dumbass. Tokyo? Do you have any idea how far that is from Hokkaido? And how much a ticket on the train costs? Oy, and how the hell am I going to get out of teaching that day? Oh, you dollface, you duckie!

CHUTES&LADDERS. I'll be wearing a jean jacket and a Padres cap. That's how you'll know me.

ORANGUTAN. Oh Chutes&Ladders. You old bag of bones, you! You old so-and-so, you mensch, you human being! Why the hell didn't you tell me?

CHUTES&LADDERS. I'm just hoping I have the guts to get on the plane.

ORANGUTAN. Of course you're getting on that damn plane! For me you did this? *(Fountainhead logs on.)*

FOUNTAINHEAD. Hey everyone. I managed to find one computer here at the hospital that works. Odessa asked me to post a message on her behalf. She landed on "Go." Hit reset on the timer. Back to day one.

ORANGUTAN. Who's Odessa?

FOUNTAINHEAD. Sorry. Haikumom.

ORANGUTAN. What? Do you log on here just to mock us?

CHUTES&LADDERS. Hold on, is she okay?

FOUNTAINHEAD. Cardiac arrest. They said she was one hair from a coma. She hadn't used in six years and her system went nuts.

CHUTES&LADDERS. So she's alive?

FOUNTAINHEAD. And just barely ticking. Tubes in and out of her nose. She's responsive, she mumbled a few words.

53

ORANGUTAN. You can't be serious.

CHUTES&LADDERS. Why are you there? Were you using with her?

FOUNTAINHEAD. No.

CHUTES&LADDERS. Did you sell her the stuff?

FOUNTAINHEAD. No, Jesus, of course not. She gave them my number, I'm her emergency contact. Why, I have no idea, we're practically strangers. Getting here to the hospital, seeing her like that … I don't mean this as an insult, but she looked not human. Bones with skin covering. Mummy-like.

ORANGUTAN. Fuck. You.

FOUNTAINHEAD. I'm being descriptive. I'm being honest. The thought of my boys walking in on me like that. My wife finding me …

ORANGUTAN. That woman is the reason I'm. Oh god, you get complacent for one second! One second! You get comfortable for one minute!

CHUTES&LADDERS. Fountainhead, does she have family there? Has anyone come through her room?

FOUNTAINHEAD. Apparently a son and a niece but they had to catch a flight to San Juan.

CHUTES&LADDERS. No parents? No other children? A friend? A neighbor?

FOUNTAINHEAD. None showed up.

CHUTES&LADDERS. Fountainhead. You have a family, I absolutely understand that, and I mean zero disrespect when I say, when I beg of you this: Your job on this earth has just changed. It's not to be a husband or a father or a CEO. It's to stay by that woman's side. Make sure she gets home safe. Bathe her. Feed her. Get her checked into a rehab, inpatient. Do not leave her side for a second. Can you do this?

FOUNTAINHEAD. I have one day clean. I'm not meant to be a saint.

CHUTES&LADDERS. Tell me now, swear on your mother's name, otherwise I'm on the first flight to Philadelphia.

FOUNTAINHEAD. I don't know.

CHUTES&LADDERS. Look man, do you believe in God?

FOUNTAINHEAD. Sure, along with unicorns and the boogeyman.

CHUTES&LADDERS. How about miracles?

FOUNTAINHEAD. When the Phils are winning.

CHUTES&LADDERS. How about actions? I bet you believe in those.

FOUNTAINHEAD. Yeah.

CHUTES&LADDERS. Your lifeboat has just arrived. Get on board or get out of the way.

FOUNTAINHEAD. I'll take care of Odessa. You have my word. My solemn word. *(Pause.)* She did manage to say one thing. Someone has to take over site admin. She doesn't want the chatroom full of curse words. *(Fountainhead's phone rings.)* I gotta go.

CHUTES&LADDERS. You gave us your word. Don't be a stranger. *(Fountainhead logs off. Into the phone.)*

FOUNTAINHEAD. Hi, honey, sorry I haven't called sooner. Listen, I'm not coming home tonight, just order in. I have a friend who got sick, she's having an emergency. No, it's not a romantic friend but she needs my help. Honey? Honey ... *(The call is over.)*

Scene 14

Puerto Rico. A hotel room. Yaz works on her laptop as a screen lights up with an icon of piano keys: FREEDOM&NOISE, STATUS: ONLINE.

FREEDOM&NOISE. Hello, I am Freedom&Noise. Current location: Rainforest B&B, Puerto Rico. This is my job app for interim site admin. Experience with chat rooms: zero. Experience with drugs: one doobie in high school. But Fountainhead said it was up to you guys if you would have me, so please hear me out. Haikumom is my aunt. For a few years she was my crazy babysitter. The baddest hide and seek player north of Girard Avenue. Dress up, booby traps, forts. Until I was eight and, poof, she disappeared. New babysitter, zero explanation. So my first Thanksgiving home from college I walk in and there's Haikumom, stuffing *pasteles* in the kitchen. Hadn't seen her in ten years. "What up, little niece? Congratulations on college." She planted a big wet one on my cheek and pulled a necklace from her shirt and said, "You know what these gold letters mean? The N is for Narcotics, the A is for Anonymous, and today is my two-year anniversary of being clean." *(Pause.)* I remember sitting next to her at that Thanksgiving table, this question first rooting itself deep in my gut. "What did I do to earn all that I have? Have I done anything difficult in my whole life?" So if you'll have me while Haikumom recovers, I'll be paying a babysitter back for all the times she let me win at Uno. Five-seven-five right? *(Counting syllables on her fingers.)* Box full of ashes … *(Elliot enters from the bathroom, freshly showered, pulling on a shirt.)*

ELLIOT. Whatchu looking at, Willis?

YAZ. Sh. I'm counting syllables. *(Elliot looks over her shoulders at the computer.)*

ELLIOT. Hold up. Don't read that shit, Yaz.

YAZ. You know how Odessa got into haiku in the first place?

ELLIOT. For real, close the computer.

YAZ. I went through this Japanese minimalist phase freshman year. Rock gardens, Zen Buddhism, the works. I gave her a haiku collection for Christmas.

ELLIOT. Yeah, and you gave me a midget tree that died by New Year's.

YAZ. Bonsai. You didn't water it.

ELLIOT. *(Closing her laptop.)* For the two days I'm away from Philly, let me be away from Philly?

YAZ. You know where I was gonna be by thirty? Two kids. Equal housework marriage. Tenure, no question. Waaaay tenured, like by the age of twenty-four. Carnegie Hall debuts Yazmin Ortiz's Oratorio for Electric Guitar and Children's Choir. I wrote a list on a piece of paper and dug a hole in Fairmount Park and put it in the ground and said, "When I turn thirty, I'll dig it up and cross it all off." And I promise you I'll never have the courage to go to that spot with a shovel and face my list full of crumbs, decoys, and Band-Aids.

ELLIOT. Married with kids, what an awful goal.

YAZ. Odessa's done things.

ELLIOT. Well, when you throw her a parade, don't expect me to come.

YAZ. You've done things.

ELLIOT. I wouldn't come to my own parade, either.

YAZ. Ginny did things. What have I done?

ELLIOT. Second-grade Language Arts. You glued my book report.

YAZ. I couldn't stop your leg from getting chewed up.

ELLIOT. Fairmount Little League basketball. You kept score, you brought our equipment.

YAZ. I didn't hold your hand when you were in the desert popping pills trying to make yourself disappear. I didn't keep Odessa away from that needle. I didn't water a single plant in Ginny's garden. We're in P.R. and I'm gonna dig a new hole and I'm not putting a wish or a list in there, I'm putting a scream in there. And I'm gonna sow it like the ugliest, foulest and most necessary seed in the world and it's going to bloom! This time it's going to fucking bloom!

ELLIOT. My eyes just did this weird thing. For a second, it was Mom standing in front of me.

YAZ. Odessa?

ELLIOT. Ginny.

YAZ. Elliot, your birth mother saved your life by giving you away. You think she's the one holding you back? Nobody can make you invisible but you. *(Yaz begins gathering her stuff hastily.)* Now we got some ashes to throw. El Yunque closes in an hour and a half.

ELLIOT. Maybe we should do this tomorrow.

YAZ. I gotta make a call. I'll be in the lobby! *(She exits.)*

ELLIOT. Yaz? *(The Ghost appears. He's probably been there the whole time.)* Yaz!

GHOST. *Momken men-fadluck ted-dini gawaz saffari? (The Ghost reaches out his hand to touch Elliot.) Momken men-fadluck ted-dini gawaz saffari? (The second they make contact, Elliot spins on his heels and grabs The Ghost. The Ghost defends himself, pulling away. They start pushing, grabbing, fighting. The Ghost is looking for something — is it Elliot's wallet?) Momken men-fadluck ted-dini gawaz saffari? (The Ghost finds Elliot's wallet and tears through it, hurling its contents onto the floor. Elliot attacks again, but this time The Ghost reaches out his hand and touches Elliot's face. Elliot freezes, unable to move, as The Ghost's hands glide across his features, considering each one with authority, taking inventory.) Momken men-fadluck ted-dini gawaz saffari? (The Ghost is gone. Elliot catches his breath, shaken. He reaches into his pocket and pulls out a bottle of pills. He puts one pill in his hand. Then he empties the entire bottle of pills into his hand. He stares at the pills, wanting to throw them away.)*

Scene 15

Split scene. Odessa's bathroom. The bathtub is filled with water. John enters, carrying a very weak Odessa. Odessa is wearing shorts and a bra, a modest outfit for bathing. John lowers her gently into the bathtub.

JOHN. Does that feel okay? *(Odessa barely nods.)* It's not too hot or cold? *(Odessa shakes her head.)* I don't know how to do this. These are things women do. Take care of sick people. Make the wounds go away. *(He takes a sponge and starts to bathe her.)* Is this okay? *(He lifts her arms and washes her armpits. Embarrassed at first, but quickly gets the swing of it.)* We check you in at 4:30 so we have plenty of time to clean you up and get you in good clothes, okay? You'll go in there looking like a decent woman. *(He stops.)* I spoke to my wife while you were sleeping. I told her to go under my bookmarks, find the website. I gave her my logon, my password. She's probably reading it right now. So you may be the only friend I have left. *(Odessa whispers something inaudible.)* What was that? *(She gestures for him to lean in. She whispers into his ear.)* One more time. *(She whispers a little louder.)* Did someone take swimming lessons? *(She whispers again.)* Did someone put on water wings? *(She nods. He continues to bathe her, gently, in silence as: Lights rise on Tokyo. Narita Airport. Orangutan sits on the floor by the luggage carousel. At her feet is a sign that says CHUTES&LADDERS. She throws the sign like a Frisbee across the floor and gets up to leave. Chutes&Ladders enters, rolling a suitcase behind him. He waves to Orangutan.)*
CHUTES&LADDERS. Orangutan?
ORANGUTAN. What the holy hell?
CHUTES&LADDERS. Sorry. Sorry. I tried calling but my cell doesn't work here. I told you I'm no good at this fancy kind of living.
ORANGUTAN. You were supposed to land yesterday, you were too scared to get on the plane. You rebook, you were supposed to land today, three hours ago. Everyone got their luggage already. The last person pulled the last suitcase from the carousel half an

hour ago. I thought, wow, this one sure knows how to play a joke on the ladies. I thought you had left me at the fucking altar.

CHUTES&LADDERS. I got sick on the flight. Totally embarrassing. I had a panic attack as the plane landed and I started tossing into the doggy bag right next to this nice old lady. I've been sitting on the bathroom floor emptying my stomach. Then I had to find a toothbrush and toothpaste and mouthwash because I didn't want to greet you with bad breath and all. *(She looks skeptical. She sniffs his mouth quickly.)*

ORANGUTAN. Minty. *(Pause.)* Oh, you dummy, you big old dummy. Put her here, you San Diego Padre. *(She extends her hand, he takes it. A long handshake. Their first physical contact.)* What's your name?

CHUTES&LADDERS. Clay. Clayton "Buddy" Wilkie.

ORANGUTAN. I'm Madeleine Mays.

CHUTES&LADDERS. It's weird, huh?

ORANGUTAN. Totally weird. The land of the living. *(They hug. They melt into each other's arms. A hug of basic survival and necessary friendship. Then, they exit, rolling his suitcase off as lights rise in: Puerto Rico. A rock outcropping looking out over a waterfall. Elliot is there, looking down at the water.)*

ELLIOT. *(Looking down.)* Oh shit! Yaz, you gotta see this! Yaz? Fucking Johnny Appleseed of El Yunque. *(Yaz enters holding a soil-covered flower bulb. She compares the root against a field book.)*

YAZ. I found my spiral ginger! This is going right next to the aloe by the kitchen door, baby!

ELLIOT. Yo, this science experiment ain't getting past security.

YAZ. Experiment my ass. I'm planting these in Ginny's garden.

ELLIOT. Customs gonna sniff that shit from a mile away.

YAZ. *(Putting the bulb in a Ziploc baggie full of dirt and bulbs.)* China rose … Seagrape … Some kind of fern …

ELLIOT. When they cuff those wrists, I don't know you.

YAZ. I'll hide them in my tampon box.

ELLIOT. That don't work. My first trip to P.R., Mami Ginny smuggled a *coqui* back with her Kotex and got arrested. Front page of the *Daily News.*

YAZ. Good shit. *(A dirty little secret.)* You know what Grandma did?

ELLIOT. Do I want to?

YAZ. She used to smuggle stuff back, too. She'd tuck it below her boobs. She had storage space under there!

ELLIOT. Yo, you think if I jumped off this rock right now and dove into that water, I'd survive?

YAZ. Just watch out for the huge boulders and the footbridge.

ELLIOT. It's tempting. That spray. *(His phone beeps.)* Reception in the rainforest.

YAZ. Kind of ruins the romance.

ELLIOT. *(Reads a text message.)* Damn, that was fast.

YAZ. What?

ELLIOT. Pop sold the house. Did he even put out a listing?

YAZ. Not that I know of.

ELLIOT. That's like a VW bus going from zero to sixty in three seconds. Don't make no sense.

YAZ. Must have been an inside job.

ELLIOT. I guess so.

YAZ. A way way inside job …

ELLIOT. Yaz …

YAZ. *(Conspiratorially.)* Yeeeees?

ELLIOT. What did you do?

YAZ. *(Very conspiratorially.)* Nothing …

ELLIOT. Holy shit!

YAZ. Put my Steinway on craigslist. Got four responses before you made it down to the lobby. My 88 keys are worth more than Ginny's whole house. Sadly. I'll buy an upright.

ELLIOT. You are one crazy motherfucking adjunct! Yo, I don't know if *el barrio* is ready for you. I don't know if they can handle you!

YAZ. Oh, they gonna handle me. It'll be the Cousins House. We'll renovate the kitchen. You redo the plumbing, I'll hook up a little tile backsplash.

ELLIOT. I watched Bob Vila with Pop, but I ain't no handyman.

YAZ. Just wait, Mr. Home Depot. You're gonna be like, *"Fuacata, fuacata, fuacata"* with your power drill and nail gun and vice grips.

ELLIOT. Something like that.

YAZ. Well? Get to it. Toss 'em.

ELLIOT. Me? Why the hell do you think I let you come along? *(He hands Yaz the box.)*

YAZ. Well then, say something. Pray.

ELLIOT. I'm all out of prayers.

YAZ. Me, too. Make a toast.

ELLIOT. To L.A.X. I'm not flying back with you.

YAZ. What do you mean?

ELLIOT. I called from the hotel and changed my flight. One way ticket. Watch out, Hollywood. *(Pause.)* You know how you had to shake me awake last night?

YAZ. *(Demeanor shifting.)* You were literally sobbing in your sleep.

ELLIOT. This dream was different than usual. I'm fixing a Subway hoagie, I feel eyes on the back of my neck, I turn around and expect to see him, the first guy I shot down in Iraq. But instead it's Mami Ginny. Standing next to the bread oven, smiling. You know how her eyes smile?

YAZ. Best smile in the world.

ELLIOT. Looking at me, her son. Coming to say goodbye.

YAZ. That's beautiful.

ELLIOT. She puts on her glasses to see my face even better. She squints and something changes. The moment I come into focus, she starts trembling. Then she starts to cry. Then she starts to scream loud, like, "Ahhh! Ahhh!" She won't stop looking at me, but she's terrified, horrified by what she sees. And I'm touching my face like, is my lip bleeding, is there a gash on my forehead? Or is she looking through my eyes and seeing straight into my fucking soul?

YAZ. Jesus.

ELLIOT. I wanted Mami Odessa to relapse, Yaz. I wanted her to pick up that needle. I knew precisely what to do, what buttons to push, I engineered that shit, I might as well have pushed the thing into her vein. Because I thought, why would God take the good one? Yo, take the bad mom instead! I was like, why wouldn't you take the bad fucking mom? If I stay in Philly, I'm gonna turn into it. I'm gonna become one of them. I'm already halfway there. You've got armor, you've got ideas, but I don't.

YAZ. Go. Go and don't you ever, ever look back. *(She takes his hand.)* But if you do, there will be a plastic-covered sofa waiting for you. *(Below them, in Philadelphia, John is done bathing Odessa. He lifts her and holds her like an angel above the bathtub. She is dripping wet and seems almost radiant, and yet deeply, deeply sick.)* I'm the elder now. I stay home. I hold down the fort.

ELLIOT. I'm walking.

YAZ. On three?

YAZ and ELLIOT. One. Two. Three. *(They toss the ashes. Blackout.)*

End of Play

PROPERTY LIST

Purse with papers, pen
Piece of paper
Business card
Coffee machine
Computers
Pad, pen
Stereo
Cell phones
Brochures
Dollar bill
Newspaper
Punching bag
Coffee mugs
Cell phone
Papers
Wallet with cash
Key
Phone
Stack of mail with rubber band
Desk phone
Calculator, pen cup
Padded envelope with deflated orange water wing
Mug of water, spoon
Flashlight
Bottle of pills
Soap, washcloth
Cardboard sign
Luggage
Flower bulb
Field guidebook
Bag of dirt and bulbs
Box of ashes

NEW PLAYS

★ **I'LL EAT YOU LAST: A CHAT WITH SUE MENGERS by John Logan.** For more than 20 years, Sue Mengers' clients were the biggest names in show business: Barbra Streisand, Faye Dunaway, Burt Reynolds, Ali MacGraw, Gene Hackman, Cher, Candice Bergen, Ryan O'Neal, Nick Nolte, Mike Nichols, Gore Vidal, Bob Fosse…If her clients were the talk of the town, she was the town, and her dinner parties were the envy of Hollywood. Now, you're invited into her glamorous Beverly Hills home for an evening of dish, dirty secrets and all the inside showbiz details only Sue can tell you. "A delectable soufflé of a solo show…thanks to the buoyant, witty writing of Mr. Logan" –NY Times. "80 irresistible minutes of primo tinseltown dish from a certified master chef." –Hollywood Reporter. [1W] ISBN: 978-0-8222-3079-3

★ **PUNK ROCK by Simon Stephens.** In a private school outside of Manchester, England, a group of highly-articulate seventeen-year-olds flirt and posture their way through the day while preparing for their A-Level mock exams. With hormones raging and minimal adult supervision, the students must prepare for their future — and survive the savagery of high school. Inspired by playwright Simon Stephens' own experiences as a teacher, PUNK ROCK is an honest and unnerving chronicle of contemporary adolescence. "[A] tender, ferocious and frightning play." –NY Times. "[A] muscular little play that starts out funny and ferocious then reveals its compassion by degrees." –Hollywood Reporter. [5M, 3W] ISBN: 978-0-8222-3288-9

★ **THE COUNTRY HOUSE by Donald Margulies.** A brood of famous and longing-to-be-famous creative artists have gathered at their summer home during the Williamstown Theatre Festival. When the weekend takes an unexpected turn, everyone is forced to improvise, inciting a series of simmering jealousies, romantic outbursts, and passionate soul-searching. Both witty and compelling, THE COUNTRY HOUSE provides a piercing look at a family of performers coming to terms with the roles they play in each other's lives. "A valentine to the artists of the stage." –NY Times. "Remarkably candid and funny." –Variety. [3M, 3W] ISBN: 978-0-8222-3274-2

★ **OUR LADY OF KIBEHO by Katori Hall.** Based on real events, OUR LADY OF KIBEHO is an exploration of faith, doubt, and the power and consequences of both. In 1981, a village girl in Rwanda claims to see the Virgin Mary. Ostracized by her schoolmates and labeled disturbed, everyone refuses to believe, until impossible happenings appear again and again. Skepticism gives way to fear, and then to belief, causing upheaval in the school community and beyond. "Transfixing." –NY Times. "Hall's passionate play renews belief in what theater can do." –Time Out [7M, 8W, 1 boy] ISBN: 978-0-8222-3301-5

DRAMATISTS PLAY SERVICE, INC.
440 Park Avenue South, New York, NY 10016 212-683-8960 Fax 212-213-1539
postmaster@dramatists.com www.dramatists.com

NEW PLAYS

★ **AGES OF THE MOON by Sam Shepard.** Byron and Ames are old friends, reunited by mutual desperation. Over bourbon on ice, they sit, reflect and bicker until fifty years of love, friendship and rivalry are put to the test at the barrel of a gun. "A poignant and honest continuation of themes that have always been present in the work of one of this country's most important dramatists, here reconsidered in the light and shadow of time passed." –NY Times. "Finely wrought…as enjoyable and enlightening as a night spent stargazing." –Talkin' Broadway. [2M] ISBN: 978-0-8222-2462-4

★ **ALL THE WAY by Robert Schenkkan. Winner of the 2014 Tony Award for Best Play.** November, 1963. An assassin's bullet catapults Lyndon Baines Johnson into the presidency. A Shakespearean figure of towering ambition and appetite, this charismatic, conflicted Texan hurls himself into the passage of the Civil Rights Act—a tinderbox issue emblematic of a divided America—even as he campaigns for re-election in his own right, and the recognition he so desperately wants. In Pulitzer Prize and Tony Award–winning Robert Schenkkan's vivid dramatization of LBJ's first year in office, means versus ends plays out on the precipice of modern America. ALL THE WAY is a searing, enthralling exploration of the morality of power. It's not personal, it's just politics. "…action-packed, thoroughly gripping… jaw-dropping political drama." –Variety. "A theatrical coup…nonstop action. The suspense of a first-class thriller." –NY1. [17M, 3W] ISBN: 978-0-8222-3181-3

★ **CHOIR BOY by Tarell Alvin McCraney.** The Charles R. Drew Prep School for Boys is dedicated to the creation of strong, ethical black men. Pharus wants nothing more than to take his rightful place as leader of the school's legendary gospel choir. Can he find his way inside the hallowed halls of this institution if he sings in his own key? "[An] affecting and honest portrait…of a gay youth tentatively beginning to find the courage to let the truth about himself become known." –NY Times. "In his stirring and stylishly told drama, Tarell Alvin McCraney cannily explores race and sexuality and the graces and gravity of history." –NY Daily News. [7M] ISBN: 978-0-8222-3116-5

★ **THE ELECTRIC BABY by Stefanie Zadravec.** When Helen causes a car accident that kills a young man, a group of fractured souls cross paths and connect around a mysterious dying baby who glows like the moon. Folk tales and folklore weave throughout this magical story of sad endings, strange beginnings and the unlikely people that get you from one place to the next. "The imperceptible magic that pervades human existence and the power of myth to assuage sorrow are invoked by the playwright as she entwines the lives of strangers in THE ELECTRIC BABY, a touching drama." –NY Times. "As dazzling as the dialogue is dreamful." –Pittsburgh City Paper. [3M, 3W] ISBN: 978-0-8222-3011-3

DRAMATISTS PLAY SERVICE, INC.
440 Park Avenue South, New York, NY 10016 212-683-8960 Fax 212-213-1539
postmaster@dramatists.com www.dramatists.com